Journey
to Moriah

Other books by Ken Wade:

Del Delker
Jesus for a New Millennium
The Orion Conspiracy

Journey to Moriah

The untold story of how Abraham became the friend of God

Ken Wade

Pacific Press® Publishing Association
Nampa, Idaho
Oshawa, Ontario, Canada
www.pacificpress.com

Designed by Dennis Ferree
Mountain photo: Michael Orton / Getty Images
Inside photo: Steve Lanto

Unless otherwise noted, all Scripture quotations are from
the New King James Version.

Additional copies of this book are available by calling toll free
1-800-765-6955 or visiting <http://www.adventistbookcenter.com>.

ISBN: 0-8163-2024-1

04 05 06 07 08 • 5 4 3 2 1

Dedication

This book is dedicated to all those who, like Abraham,
have set out to follow God and have had pause to wonder
if they somehow missed a turn along the way.

Table of Contents

Introduction:
Of Ancient History and
Modern Journeys

Writing this book has been a journey for me. I wrote and preached extensively about Abraham in the 1980s. That's when I began this manuscript. Coming back to it nearly twenty years later at the request of Pacific Press's acquisitions editor Tim Lale has been a journey of its own, revealing that my understanding of God and His leading was not stagnating while the manuscript collected dust.

Abraham's story has been a guiding light for my life since the earliest days of my spiritual journey—but not always in positive ways, because I sometimes got things backwards. Stories ought to be read forward. I don't like to peek ahead at the last chapter of a book to find out how everything comes out. To have its best effect, a story must unfold page by page, and journeys too should proceed forward. There's a reason we can't see the future: because we need to live life one day at a time and learn our lessons one at a time. It wasn't until I came to see Abraham's life as a journey toward a destination, unknown to him but known to us from countless tellings, that the true meaning of his life story came clear.

Please join me on a journey with Abraham to Mt. Moriah. We'll try to see it through his eyes, so we can learn the lessons he did as he went along. Life is a journey, and the more we can learn on the way, the better. In the end, if we've learned to trust God as Abraham did, the purpose of the telling of his story will have been fulfilled.

In the first part of our journey, we'll delve extensively into the historical, religious, and social background of Abraham's life. If you're interested in more detailed information about the historical background of the story, particularly how the Bible's timeline based on genealogies fits into archaeological history, take a moment to read the brief historical appendix at the end of the book before you start chapter 1. One more note before we begin: For the sake of simplicity I have chosen to use the names *Abraham* and *Sarah* all through this book, though they bore the names *Abram* and *Sarai* till Abraham was ninety-nine years old.

CHAPTER ONE

The God of Abraham

" 'Thus says the LORD God of Israel: "Your fathers, including Terah, the father of Abraham and the father of Nahor, dwelt on the other side of the River in old times; and they served other gods" ' "
(Joshua 24:2).

At the beginning of my spiritual journey, I became fascinated with one particular part of Abraham's journey. The end. The Akedah, as it's called. The binding of Isaac. The story's meaning was clear to me. It meant that God wanted me to be willing to give up the thing dearest to my heart.

I struggled with that, always trying to fulfill the ideal I saw in Abraham. His story constantly warned me not to get too attached to anything for fear that God would ask me to give it up. I gave up meals and fasted. I gave up desserts when I ate. I gave up pursuit of peer acclaim and popularity. In a particularly painful episode of trying to bring myself totally into harmony with God's will, I convinced myself that I had to quit courting my fiancée—after all, she was the dearest thing to me, so God must want me to give her up! Fortunately, more experienced Christians helped me to see that wasn't necessarily God's plan. I've now been happily married to her for more than thirty years.

I think I had a fixation on the Akedah. I thought that the only way I could really prove that God was first in my life was to let Him (actually, to *make* Him) take away everything I wanted most. Had I

JOURNEY TO MORIAH

been raised a Roman Catholic, I probably would have become a monk.

Looking back, I know I was wrong—that I had gotten the wrong message about God by dwelling so much on one part of one story instead of seeing Abraham's journey as a whole. To me, the story's message was that God is a taker. Somehow I completely missed the crux of the account, which Abraham himself expressed: "God will *provide.*"

The story of the binding of Isaac is worth dwelling on. It is one of the most powerful stories in the Bible, and it foreshadows God's own sacrifice of His Son for the salvation of the world. It can engender the courage to go on no matter how steep the path. It can give us the faith to entrust our future to God. But it is not intended as a pattern for a beginning pilgrim. It came at the end of Abraham's journey. It was a final exam, just before graduation—not an opening-day exercise. By the time the old man Abraham arrived at Mt. Moriah, God had already had him in the classroom for over a century. Abraham had passed and failed myriad smaller tests and pop quizzes along the way—as part of his preparation for the big final on Mt. Moriah. So let's go back to the beginning of Abraham's life and follow him step by step as he learns to walk with and trust God.

THE GODS OF THE LAND

Abraham was raised in the very shadow of one of the premier holy places of ancient religion. The great ziggurat at Ur in southern Mesopotamia (modern Iraq) was the center of worship of the moon god, who was known as Nanna when the moon was full, as Sin when the moon was a crescent, and as Asimbabbar when the new moon was just a sliver in the western sky after sunset.

The ziggurat measured 150 by 200 feet at the base and rose in three tiers to a height of seventy or eighty feet. It was built of handmade mud bricks—sun-dried ones at its core and kiln-fired ones sealed with bitumen on the surface. None of the bricks was much more than 15 inches long, so if you do the math, you know the people who built that ziggurat had to make millions of bricks. Obviously, worship was very important to them.

The God of Abraham

Archaeologist André Parrot explains that

> the ziggurat forms a gigantic pedestal designed to facilitate the descent of the gods to the earth. No pains were spared to provide a place of reception worthy of the celestial visitant. A temple of welcome stood at the top of the tower, and a second shrine [stood] at ground level to accommodate the god during his sojourn. The two were connected by stairways along which processions mounted and descended, and which formed, as it were, a permanent line of communication between heaven and earth.[1]

Hmmm . . . Sounds a bit like a dream that Abraham's grandson Jacob had, doesn't it? (See Genesis 26.) Do you suppose that when Jacob dreamed of a "ladder" to heaven, what he actually saw in his mind's eye was a ziggurat? I know that's not the way they show it in Bible storybooks for kids, but I've always found it helpful to try to picture the Bible stories within their original setting instead of assuming that people who lived four thousand years ago saw things the same way I do. The word translated *ladder* can equally well be translated *stairway.* One thing's sure: Jacob didn't dream about an aluminum extension ladder like the one I keep in my garage!

How do you suppose the people who lived where Abraham grew up pictured their gods? Remember, we're talking about a time thirty-five hundred years before Michelangelo decorated the ceiling of the Sistine Chapel with a painting of a bearded old-man God stretching out His finger to Adam. The concept of God that Abraham had in mind at the beginning of his journey wasn't God as we picture Him today. When Abraham set out to know God, he had a lot of learning—and considerable unlearning—to do along the way.

For one thing, he didn't know God's name as *Yahweh, Jehovah,* or the LORD. That's very clear from Exodus 6:2, 3: "God spoke to Moses and said to him: 'I am the LORD. I appeared to Abraham, to Isaac, and to Jacob as God Almighty, but by My name, LORD [*Jehovah,* or *Yahweh*], I was not known to them.'" Bible scholars have pointed out that none of the early patriarchs had names that incorporated the name *Yahweh/Jehovah* (such as "*Jeho*shaphat," "*Jeho*ram," and "*Jeho*shua"—Joshua). Names like these don't appear until the time of the Exodus.

Of course as you read the story of Abraham in Genesis, you'll find the name of the LORD mentioned often. Genesis 12:8 even says that Abraham built an altar to the LORD and "called on the name of the LORD." The original Hebrew says he called on the name of Yahweh. And later, he even names a place "The LORD will provide" (commonly rendered "Jehovah-Jireh," see Genesis 22).

How can we handle this seeming contradiction? If Exodus says God didn't reveal His name Yahweh/Jehovah to Abraham, how could the patriarch name a place Jehovah-Jireh?

This seems to be a clear instance of a later storyteller filling in information that wasn't available at the time the events happened. When Moses wrote Genesis, he understood that Abraham had been communicating with the LORD all along, so when he told the story, he filled in the correct name for God—even though Abraham actually called on God by a different name, such as "God Most High" (*El Elyon*) or "God Almighty" (*El Shaddai*)—the name by which the LORD introduced Himself in the story told in Genesis 17. Abraham probably named the place mentioned in Genesis 22 *El-Jireh,* but later generations knew it as *Jehovah-Jireh.* Reading through Abraham's story and seeing the different names by which God is identified makes quite an interesting study. It seems clear that the process of getting to know God included learning to know Him by different names.

The Bible also makes it very plain that Abraham was a product of his polytheistic environment. Somehow, growing up, I got the impression that Abraham had been raised in a godly home, where knowledge of the one true God of Israel had been preserved, and no one even looked at idols or other gods. But that's just not biblical. Years later, Joshua recorded the Lord as saying, " ' "Your fathers, including Terah, the father of Abraham and the father of Nahor, dwelt on the other side of the River in old times; and they served other gods" ' " (Joshua 24:2).

The God of Abraham

Let's face it. To really understand the story of Abraham and learn his life lessons with him, we may have to abandon some of our preconceived notions. We need to try to see the world as he saw it.

NANNA, THE MOON GOD

To begin with, it seems safe to assume that one of the gods Terah and his family served was the moon—known as Nanna. But to see the moon as they saw it, we need to erase a lot of imagery from our minds. When they looked up at the night sky, they didn't see a huge rocky sphere cruising around the earth, captivated by the gravity of the planet they were living on. No, what they saw was a mystifying source of light in the sky. One unlike any other. One that waxed and waned and regularly disappeared entirely, only to reappear again and grow. Sometimes though, when it was at full strength, it was attacked—partially or wholly eaten away by some mysterious, obviously evil, power. What we see as an eclipse, they saw as demons attacking their god. In some Sumerian cities the priests would beat a huge drum, nearly six feet in diameter, during an eclipse to scare the demons away.

When Nanna was growing, he chased the sun (the god known as Utu) across the sky, their chariots hastening daily from horizon to horizon, drawn by some immense, invisible, but tireless asses or oxen. And when Nanna reached full size, he would claim the eastern horizon at the precise moment when Utu was sinking below the ground in the west. Then, for one glorious, triumphant night each month, Nanna would rule supreme, riding majestically across the sky, sole lord of heaven and earth, a cowherd cruising among his herd of stars.

On the very next night, however, Nanna would come tardy to the scene, leaving earth dark and moonless for nearly an hour. And each night from then on he would appear later and be weaker and smaller, now having to run for dear life from Utu, who pursued him. Finally, having lost the chariot race across the sky, Nanna would once again disappear, gone to the nether world with Utu. Usually there would be three nights per month when Nanna was totally absent from the sky. During that time, Ur's priests would conduct special religious ceremonies at the ziggurat, seeking to ensure that the city's chief god would have the strength to return from the netherworld.

On the fourth night, the priests would wait eagerly, watching as Utu sank beneath the horizon. They would gaze in his direction, waiting to see if Nanna had survived. Would he return? Then, as daylight faded, without fail, month after month, year after year, and century after century, from their sky-high perches atop ziggurats spread all across the wide, flat plains of Mesopotamia, priests would see it: the sign of Nanna appearing in the sky perhaps half an hour after the sun had gone to the netherworld. Just a little, short-lived thumbnail of light that first night—but one that gave the sign of their god: the crescent shape of the horns of a bull. Yes! Nanna, their great bull, their protector in the sky, had survived. He had returned from the underworld, where he had been spending his time with Utu and other gods, passing judgment on the deeds done on earth.

Nanna and Utu were not the only gods known to Abraham and his kin. Enki, the god of fresh water, flowed in the Tigris and Euphrates rivers and in the canals, bringing life to the soil and fish for the eating to the residents of the land defined by the two rivers. Enki was a wise, usually beneficent god who was known for his ability to circumvent the scheming of other gods in ways that would benefit humanity. Like water you try to dam up, Enki could always find a way around whatever obstacles might be thrown in his path.

But even for a god so wise, life was not always easy. Sometimes he ran his course with great strength (in the spring). But just like Nanna, he sometimes faded into near non-existence (in the fall). Fortunately, he could almost always count on the great air god Enlil and the storm god Ishkur to bring the spring rains and revive his strength. It was then, at the beginning of the year, that Enki would team up with Nanna to bring the spring floods and their accompanying runs of carp to feed the people of Ur.

Observing this today, we would say that the spring runoff from the mountains coincided with an especially high tide brought on by the full moon, and that these two events often happened about the time the carp, which spend most of the winter in near-hibernation on the bottom of the river, were coming up for their spring mating run. But the ancients didn't have satellite images that revealed what was happening at the headwaters of the Euphrates in Turkey. They'd heard that the two great rivers of Mesopotamia flowed from the eye sockets of the slain goddess Tiamat. Nor did they understand the law of gravity that causes tides. And when the carp went to their winter rest down on the bottom of the river, they basically disappeared from the fisherman's world. If the fish reappeared in spring when both Nanna and Enki were at full strength, then the gods ought to get credit for it! In an ancient song, Enki proclaims:

> When I draw near unto heaven the rains of abundance
>   rain down from above,
> when I draw near unto the earth, the carp-flood at its height
>   comes into being,
> when I draw near unto the yellowing fields,
>   grain piles are heaped at my command.[2]

In the world as Abraham knew it, almost everything that happened in nature had a divine cause. When the hills and valleys turned green in spring and brown in the summer, it wasn't because of the movement of high and low pressure areas over the North Atlantic or different patterns in the flow of the jet stream. Things greened up in the spring because Dumuzi (later known as Tammuz, see Ezekiel 8:14), the god of fertility and vegetation, had been let out of the prison cell in the underworld where he had to spend much of the year. The thunderstorms that formed up against distant mountain ranges didn't result from moisture condensing out of the air as it rose and cooled. They resulted from the storm god going to war against the god of the mountains, shooting fiery arrows and bellowing like a bull or roaring like a lion. And the rivers that ran red with mud after a storm were full of the blood that had been shed in the battle.

JOURNEY TO MORIAH

How much of this polytheistic mythology Abraham had absorbed we can't know. Nor can we assess how much of Noah's knowledge of the real origin of the earth had been passed down to Abraham. All we know is that by the time of Terah, Abraham's father, humankind's vision of God the Creator was pretty mixed up. And God wanted to do something about that.

Scholars have analyzed the religion revealed in the multitude of clay tablets that have been found in Mesopotamia. They attribute the development of knowledge of a personal god to that part of the world. In fact, the idea that a great god would strike up a friendship with a single individual first appears in the very area where Abraham lived and about the time that he lived. Isn't that fascinating? Surely Noah and his sons knew that God cared about them individually. But that knowledge was lost to humankind for many years. It took a man like Abraham to rediscover it.

So, how did God get through to Abraham? That's what the story of the journey to Moriah is all about.

---

1. André Parrot, *Sumer: The Dawn of Art,* Stuart Gilbert and James Emmons, trans. (New York: Golden Press, 1961), 201.

2. Thorkild Jacobsen, *The Treasures of Darkness* (New Haven: Yale University Press, 1976), 110.

CHAPTER TWO

First
Contact

"Terah took his son Abram and his grandson Lot,
the son of Haran, and his daughter-in-law Sarai,
his son Abram's wife, and they went out with them
from Ur of the Chaldeans to go to the land of
Canaan; and they came to Haran and dwelt there"
(Genesis 11:31).

How did it all begin—the journey that would take Abraham to the peak of one of the highest spiritual mountains ever climbed?

I've heard people tell the story in a way that makes Abraham a great man of faith from the get-go. They picture him in Ur, kneeling down and calling on the name of the Lord amidst the babble of pagan idolaters. They tell of his decision to take his family away from all that—to answer the call of God and go to Canaan. The problem is, that's not the way the Bible tells the story, and it seems to me we ought to let the Bible speak for itself. So that's what we'll do. We'll be looking at Abraham's story as it is told in Genesis, with reference to outside sources when they shed light that can help us understand the story.

Genesis 11:31 says, "Terah took his son Abram and his grandson Lot, the son of Haran, and his daughter-in-law Sarai, his son Abram's wife, and they went out with them from Ur of the Chaldeans to go to the land of Canaan; and they came to Haran and dwelt there." There's no mention of Abraham's involvement in the decision. When the deacon Stephen tells the story (see Acts 7), he implies that Abraham answered God's call while in Ur, reflecting a later understanding of Abraham's journey. But Genesis, the original source of the story, says nothing about Abraham hearing the call of God in Ur. Terah is the one who plans the move. As far as we know, Abraham just went along with what the rest of the clan was doing. At that time, even more than now, it was important to stick with your family. Families were tight-knit and under the control of the oldest male. Individual freedom wasn't valued nearly as highly as family unity and prosperity.

The Terah family most likely was involved in the import-export business. Ur was ideally situated for a family involved in that profession, and so was Haran, as I'll show later. Ur was the first port of call for ships sailing up the Euphrates River from the Persian Gulf.

The city fathers in Ur had done everything they could to facilitate trade. I've seen an artist's conception of what the city might have looked like in its heyday. What amazed me most was the fact that the city wasn't actually adjacent to the Euphrates; instead, canals deep enough to accommodate ships had been dug to connect Ur with the river. One canal actually passed through the wall on the west side of town, allowing ships to sail right through the city and anchor in one of the two safe harbors inside the walls! (I should note that this painting is somewhat speculative in its interpretation of the ruins of Ur. Other archaeologists' sketches don't go so far as to show harbors inside the walls; they just leave those areas blank.)

There's no doubt that Ur was a major trading center. I think it's safe to say that it was the New York City of its day. The population was probably about thirty thousand, which made it a giant metropolis for that time. No doubt the city was filled with busy marketplaces where goods arriving from points south could be traded for those coming from the north.

Before Abraham's birth, in the time of the Ur III Dynasty, safe land and river trade routes had been established all the way up the Euphrates River into central Turkey to the north, and ships from Ur would travel nearly a thousand miles south to a place called Magan (modern-day Oman) at the mouth of the Persian Gulf. Magan served as a transshipment point for goods going to and coming from the Harappan civilization, another thousand miles away on the Indus River in modern Pakistan.

Goods coming from the south would include copper ore and tin for making bronze, diorite stone for carving statues, pearls from the gulf, timber, gold, and beautiful blue lapis lazuli gemstones that had been mined in Afghanistan and shipped via the Harappan cities in Pakistan. (Afghanistan was also a source of tin.) In exchange for these items, the Mesopotamian merchants would ship wool, cloth, silver, copper, fat, resin, and grain.

Temple records have been found that indicate that in the years just prior to the northward journey of Terah and company, trade was under the control of the priesthood at the temple. Temples in those days served as banks as well as places to worship the gods. Tithe receipts have been found among the ruins of the temple in Ur. When Ur's farmers, fishermen, and merchants brought their goods into town to sell, the priests were the first people to get a cut of the produce. Tithes were stored in the temple and used as capital to finance trading expeditions up the river and down the gulf, and other commercial ventures as well. One tablet reveals that the priests' holdings at one time included 40,000 sheep!

But the religious establishment's fortunes tended to rise and fall with the political well-being of the city. When Amorite raiders and Elamite warriors overran the city during Terah's early years, the priests and their god were held responsible. What had brought this great disaster on the proud city that had once ruled all the land between the Tigris and Euphrates—modern Iraq and parts of Syria? Why hadn't Nanna delivered them from their attackers? Had he become too old and feeble to defend them?

THE "LAMENT FOR UR"

The ancients believed that their gods were responsible for everything that happened. So, when one city triumphed over another, there had to be a divine explanation. And that explanation is given in a long hymn (it fills thirty large clay tablets!) called the "Lament for Ur," which archaeologists discovered in the ruins of Ur and Nippur, another ancient city.

This hymn explains that the gods met in council at Nippur because that city housed the main temple of the mighty god Enlil—god of the air and winds. In Abraham's day, Enlil was regarded as sort of a chief executive officer; no god could do anything without his permission. Nanna, chief god of Ur, was subject to Enlil's will. In fact, every year in the spring, one of the chief duties of the king and priests of Ur was to prepare a barge loaded with milk, cream, cheese, and other produce from their city and send it, along with a statue of Nanna, on a seven-day journey up the canals to Nippur. The details of this journey are revealed in another ancient hymn, known as "The Journey of Nanna to Nippur."

The gods often convened councils at Nippur to decide what to do. One of the things the gods discussed when they met was who among the humans should be king. According to the "Lament for Ur," after the dynasty we know as Ur III had ruled the earth for about a hundred years, the gods decided that was long enough. The "Lament" pictures Ningal—goddess wife of Nanna—pleading with Enlil and with An, the father of all the gods:

> I dragged my feet and I stretched out my arms,
> truly I shed my tears in front of An.
> Truly I myself mourned in front of Enlil:
>
> "May my city not be destroyed!"
>   I said indeed to them.
> "May Ur not be destroyed!" I said indeed to them.
> "And may its people not be killed!"
>   I said indeed to them.
> But An never bent towards those words,
> and Enlil never with an, "It is pleasing, so be it!"
>   did soothe my heart.
>
> (Behold,) they gave instruction
>   that the city be destroyed,
> (behold,) they gave instruction
>   that Ur be destroyed,
> and its destiny decreed
>   that its inhabitants be killed.[1]

Somehow Nanna and Ningal had lost rank among the gods, and as a result their city fell prey to its attackers. This must have led to a loss of prestige for their priests as well. Maybe people quit bringing their tithes and offerings when the gods no longer provided protection. Certainly the temple treasury was raided and emptied by the invaders. In the aftermath, the priesthood lost control of Wall Street. The cuneiform tablets from Ur reveal that in the years after the fall of Ur, people who wanted to mount a trading expedition up the river or send a fleet of ships down to Magan no longer looked to the temple for financing. Control of trade was taken over by several of the leading families in town. Was Terah's family one of those leading financiers?

On the other hand, the raid on Ur and the sacking of the temple demonstrated to all the city's residents, including Terah, that Nanna was no longer a dependable defender. Political events often throw theology into turmoil—witness, for example, the decline of religion and rise of agnosticism and atheism in Europe in the years following World War II. This has in part been attributed to Europeans' sense that their prayers and religious behavior did not protect them from the horrendous atrocities of that conflict. In fact, those who stood up to Hitler in the name of God and religion often received the worst treatment.

In Abraham's day, if one god didn't work out for you, then you could always try another. However, not worshiping any god at all doesn't seem to have occurred to people of that era. Maybe some of the people of Ur turned their allegiance to Enlil at this time, or Enki, the god whose power flowed in the river. And Terah? Maybe the tragedy at Ur was just the medicine he needed to turn his thoughts back toward his spiritual roots.

THE GODS BECOME PERSONAL

As I mentioned in chapter 1, it was at this precise time in history that the written records we have reveal that men and women began to think differently about the divine powers around them. In all of written history up to this time (which of course excludes the time immediately after the Flood, from which no written materials have been preserved), no one had dared to think of the gods as taking a personal interest in individuals. In fact, according to the Sumerian creation epic, the gods created people mainly because they were tired of doing all the work of dredging the canals.

The Euphrates and Tigris rivers both carry a lot of silt, which quickly filled up and blocked the canals that were necessary for agriculture, necessitating their regular cleaning. So the story Sumerian children were told when they asked their parents where people came from had nothing to do with a loving Creator placing their first parents in a bountiful garden to enjoy its delights. Far from it. The story involved a divine labor dispute that led to a strike. It seems that all the junior gods had been serving Enlil faithfully throughout eternity, but that he was a pretty harsh taskmaster. One day the gods were fed up with all their toil, and they got together, formed a labor union, and burned their tools. Then they told Enlil they weren't going to work anymore. So, Enlil and the other gods oversaw the creation of human beings and then handed them the tools they would need to keep the canals clean and raise food for themselves and the gods.

There was no love lost between the gods and their people or the people and their gods. Yes, the people would bring tithes, offerings, and sacrifices to the temple—but not because they loved their god; only because that's what was required of them. In exchange for these gifts, the people could make special requests of the god of their city or some other god.

Cylinder seals reveal a lot about life in biblical times. Many of the thousands of them that have been found bear scenes of religious significance—with a worshiper or supplicant approaching a god with an offering. The person in the picture is usually a king, and in pictures from before the time of Abraham, the king is usually accompanied by a goddess, who seems to be serving as the king's mediator as he approaches Nanna or Utu or some other great god. The goddess usually stands between the worshiper and the god. About the time of Abraham, however, the art on some seals changed. These seals picture the goddess standing *behind* the supplicant, which may indicate a theological shift toward seeing the gods as more approachable.

First Contact

About this time as well, two new forms of literature developed. In the type known as "Penitential Psalms," the writers acknowledge, in light of their current woes, that they must have done something to offend the god, and then ask their personal deity to point out their sin and to absolve them and bless them once again.

In a similar type of literature called "Letters to Gods," the writers tell their personal deity about their problems and appeal for redress. Compare the following passage from a letter addressed to the god Enki with King David's great penitential hymn in Psalm 51:

> Today let me take my trespasses to you,
>   snatch me from my foes,
> and when you have seen where I fell,
>   take pity on me,
> When you have turned my dark stretches
>   (of road) into daylight
> let me pass through your gate,
>   which releases from sin and wrongdoings,
>   let me sing your praises,
> let me confess, (roaring) like a bull,
>   my trespasses to you,
>   and let me tell of your greatness.[2]

The author of this poem, a scribe named Suen-shamuh, clearly expects his personal god, Enki, to do something about his problems (turn his dark stretches to light), and he plans to sing his god's praises once that has happened.

What we're witnessing in the art and literature of Mesopotamia from the time of Abraham is a theological renaissance. Out of the dark ages of belief in impersonal gods who care about humans only as slaves is being reborn an awareness that God is concerned about individuals. And the story of Abraham is Exhibit One of how this came about.

It seems likely that Terah's turn back toward his spiritual roots may have been what persuaded him to lead his family out of Ur and head for Canaan. There's no evidence that God actually spoke to him there, or

JOURNEY TO MORIAH

called him. The call comes later, up in Haran, and is addressed to Abraham. Considering how the story turns out, though, I can't help but think that when the family headed out from Ur, there was a spiritual hunger driving them toward Canaan.

Often a first contact with God takes this form. There's no audible voice. No lights flash. No bells ring. But somehow, due to a personal crisis or a sense of longing for something more in life, people begin a journey. They become restless, begin making changes in their life. They may not even realize at first that they've begun a journey toward God. Nonetheless, the Holy Spirit is there, watching, waiting for the right opportunity to lead them a step further, and then another step further, until the journey becomes a genuine spiritual quest—a longing, a hunger, a thirst, an urgency to find God and to follow Him wherever He may lead.

My own spiritual journey began that way. I didn't set out to find God. In fact I had turned my back and was running away from Him. Then I bumped into what seemed to my young mind like a catastrophe. As I bounced off that obstacle in my life, God was waiting, and I bumped into Him as well.

Maybe that's happened to you, too. Or maybe it will happen some day. If you're facing a disaster right now—well, maybe this is your time of opportunity. Maybe you're ready for a trip to Canaan.

But let me warn you. The road ahead is likely to be bumpy.

It was for Abraham and his kin.

---

1. Thorkild Jacobsen, *The Treasures of Darkness* (New Haven: Yale University Press, 1976), 88.

2. Ibid., 154.

CHAPTER THREE

The Long Road
to Canaan

"Noah awoke from his wine, and knew what his
younger son had done to him. Then he said:
'Cursed be Canaan; a servant of servants he shall
be to his brethren.... May God enlarge Japheth,
and may he dwell in the tents of Shem; and may
Canaan be his servant' " (Genesis 9:24-27).

"Why Canaan, Terah? What would make you choose Canaan as the destination for your family? Did you see travel brochures touting its charms? You've got to be careful of those things—they only show pictures of the prettiest places and the finest resorts. Life in Canaan won't be anything like what you're accustomed to in Ur. You're a city boy, and you're headed for the country. Do you think you'll be able to handle the culture shock?" I can hear Terah's neighbors putting questions like these to their friend when he started loading up the family donkeys and announced where he was going.

How much awareness of the ideas we find in Genesis do you suppose Terah had? Moses didn't write these things down until almost five centuries later. Had that phrase about the descendants of Canaan being the servants of Shem's offspring come down through the family to Abraham? He was, after all, a Semite—a descendant of Shem. Did he remember the words of Noah and figure that if he moved to Canaan, God would provide him with a whole retinue of servants? Even though we don't believe in slavery and hate to think of a whole race of people being subjugated to another race simply because of something an ancient ancestor did, the world Terah and Abraham inhabited saw things that way. And we're trying to see the story through their eyes.

We can't know for sure what motivated Terah to select Canaan for his next home. All we know is that when he led his family out of Ur, that's where he headed. And it would be quite a journey. I wonder how well he understood just how much of a trip he was undertaking.

If he was involved in the import-export business in Ur, he no doubt talked with traders who regularly made the journey north into Turkey and northwest into Canaan. So I'm sure he wasn't totally in the dark about what he was setting out to do. Who knows, maybe he had made the journey a few times himself. Still, it would be a rugged, challenging trip—far more difficult with a family in tow than with an experienced, travel-hardened group of caravaners.

We're not talking about going out to the driveway, piling the wife, kids, and cousins into the Winnebago, gassing up at Costco, and hitting the Interstate highways here. We're talking about loading whatever of your possessions will fit, along with provisions for the journey, on the backs of as many donkeys and camels as you can afford, and inviting your extended family, young and old alike, to put their sandals and walking sticks to good use from sunup to sundown every day for the next several months.

"Every day?" you say. "Surely Abraham and company stopped and rested on the Sabbath!"

Maybe so. But you never find any mention of the Sabbath in stories about Abraham and his immediate descendants. Remember, we're dealing with people who've lost much of their knowledge of true religion. They're just relearning it now, step by step. And even four hundred years later, God had to *remind* His people to *remember* the Sabbath—as something they'd apparently forgotten (Exodus 20:8).

Terah and his family probably had to link up with a caravan in order to travel safely. Assyrian records from this era reveal that most traders had about twenty donkeys, but they would join together with others to form caravans of up to two hundred donkeys. When you travel in a caravan, you have to move when the caravan moves and stop when the caravan stops. It must have been something like the journey west on the Oregon Trail, but without the wagons. The route Terah and company had to follow was too rough for wagons. Most wagon trains averaged about fifteen miles a day. That's probably what caravans could do in ancient Mesopotamia as well.

FOUR MONTHS OF WALKING

In *Archaeological History of the Ancient Middle East,* Jack Finegan reports that a record has come down to us from the time of Hammurabi, in the century after Terah and Abraham's journey, of a military expedition. It started

> from Larsa, not far from Ur, [went] up the Euphrates to Babylon and Sippar, up the Tigris to Ashur and beyond, then across the headwaters of the Khabur to Haran and on to Emar in Syria, at the bottom of the great bend of the Euphrates. Judging from the days of march and the distances involved, the trip was made at a speed of twenty-five to thirty kilometers per day; with stops and layovers, the outbound journey took 87 days, the return 107 days.[1]

And Canaan was farther yet—Shechem in central Canaan was at least another 360 miles (576 kilometers). At twenty-five kilometers a day, that's more than three weeks of walking! We're talking about a lot of sandal leather and way too many blisters! Traveling with a family, it must have taken a good four months of walking. It seems doubtful that many family members had the luxury of riding a donkey or camel. Those beasts of burden would have been needed to carry possessions, trade items, and provisions.

If you look at a map, you'll see that Jerusalem is almost due west of Ur. If a person could go the way the crow flies, it would be a trip of only about 650 miles. But the land between is almost entirely trackless, waterless desert. No one crossed that wilderness in those days, and few people do even today.

The preferred route in Abraham's time followed the Euphrates as far as Sippar (the point just south of modern Baghdad where the Tigris and

Euphrates come closest together), then followed the Tigris to join the major east-west road at Ashur for the trip westward to Canaan via Haran. Historians think that a shorter route—following the Euphrates all the way—was probably considered too dangerous in the years immediately following the collapse of the Ur III Dynasty. The route up the Tigris was maintained and protected by the Assyrians of northern Mesopotamia, who had established at least twenty trading outposts in central Turkey.

Browsing through the history section of a used bookstore one day, I came upon an ancient-looking book called *With Star and Crescent* by an American identified only as A. Locher. (I wonder if his name was Abraham?) The book, first published in 1888, contains one of the most fascinating true stories I've ever read. Its subtitle proclaims that it is "A FULL AND AUTHENTIC ACCOUNT OF A RECENT JOURNEY WITH A CARAVAN FROM BOMBAY TO CONSTANTINOPLE, COMPRISING A DESCRIPTION OF THE COUNTRY, THE PEOPLE, AND INTERESTING ADVENTURES WITH THE NATIVES." Interesting indeed!

I was especially intrigued by Mr. A. Locher's account of traveling in a caravan from Baghdad up through northern Mesopotamia on a trail that probably followed much the same route that Terah and company took eons earlier. Traveling conditions had not changed much in the four millennia that passed between A. Terah's and A. Locher's trips—except that people didn't ride horses in Abraham's day. That development wouldn't come for at least another thousand years. In fact, Abraham may never have seen a horse. Apparently, they were introduced to the Middle East about 2000 B.C.

What about camels? Well, there is even some dispute as to whether the camel had been domesticated by the time of the patriarchs. The scholars on the "nay" side of the argument point out that these humped beasts are seldom mentioned in texts recovered from that era. They believe that as the story was passed down orally through the years, camels were added by some storyteller who assumed that because camels were used in his day, they must have been in Abraham's day as well. Those on the "yea" side point out that domesticated camels are mentioned in a cuneiform text from the nineteenth century B.C. that was found at the site of ancient Ugarit in Syria. In addition, a figure of a kneeling camel from the same era was found at Byblos, also in Syria. The best reading of the evidence seems to support the idea that domesticated camels didn't come into common usage until several centuries later, but that those who argue against the authenticity of the stories of the patriarchs on the basis of anachronisms—details that don't fit with the actual time of the story—are probably overstating their case.

Assuming that Abraham did own camels places him in a rather elite group. Maybe if he had lived today, he would have been chauffeured about in a Rolls Royce or driven his own Lamborghini. Or maybe the best analogy would be that he would have a private helicopter to take him from place to place!

NOT A PRETTY PICTURE

Reading A. Locher's account of the stifling heat, ubiquitous fleas and sand flies, precipitous trails, and other hardships of the journey gave me a whole new appreciation for what God was asking Terah and Abraham to do when He invited them to set out on a pilgrimage. I guess I originally pictured the troupe traveling beside a peaceful river, stopping each evening in verdant pastures to let the sheep and cattle graze while the womenfolk prepared mutton roast and barley cakes under the shade of a majestic oak tree.

Maybe I got that picture from some Bible storybook I read sometime, I don't know. But if you watched any of the news reports from Iraq during the 2003 war there, you probably realize that the terrain Abraham and Terah crossed was far less idyllic than that. The following passage from *With Star and Crescent,* which describes Locher's first night after leaving Baghdad, is probably fairly representative of the type of conditions the patriarchal travelers had to put up with on a daily basis as they made their way to Haran.

A short twilight gave place to a beautiful clear, moonlight night, though it was disagreeably sultry; owing to the oppressive atmosphere, and the heavily laden pack horses, the caravan advanced but slowly. My two friends and myself therefore informed Signor P. that, in order not to fall asleep, we would ride ahead of the party, and see if there would be room for [two] caravans in the Khan of Dsheddeidah. We . . . found the [inn-keeper] stretched to his full length on the bare ground, snoring lustily. A good sound shake brought him back to consciousness, whereupon we told him that we wanted food and water for ourselves and horses, and that a whole caravan would arrive before long. He seemed totally indifferent to the news, quietly remarking that he had nothing to eat himself; but as for water there was plenty of it in the river close by. On examination, however, we found the stream at this place lay between perpendicular banks, over fifteen feet in height, and quite inaccessible for camels and horses and there was no bucket or vessel of any kind in the deserted caravansary for carrying water. We were told that there was no other water to be had in the neighborhood, nor a handful of mashed straw nor barley, the usual food for horses all over Arabia and Mesopotamia, nor any human food to be had in the place. . . . [After some rather harsh persuasion, the khanjee finally] went out, and woke another Arab . . . and told him to show us the way to the swamp. Reluctantly and slowly the fellow obeyed, and telling us to follow him with our horses to the water, he led us into a dense thicket of reeds, and brushwood, rendered still more gloomy by the shadows of a cluster of date trees surrounding it, in the centre of which lay a small, but very deep pool, or rather swamp, the water of which could not have been of the best quality, as the horses refused to drink, and soon began to plunge energetically, almost succeeding in pitching us out of our saddles and into the swamp. This was owing chiefly to the mosquitoes, which assailed us furiously on every side, causing us to beat a hasty retreat. Our horses, however, most mysteriously continued kicking and plunging all the way to the khan, and it was not before we were about taking off their saddles that we discovered that their legs and lower parts were covered with leeches. . . . [We] lay down to sleep with our saddles for pillows unmindful of the clouds of mosquitoes dancing horn-pipes on our faces.[2]

The Long Road to Canaan

A few years later, in 1889, the University of Pennsylvania sponsored the first American archaeological expedition to Mesopotamia. The archaeologists headed out from Aleppo in Syria, traveling in a camel caravan to Nippur in southern Mesopotamia. Along the way they encountered blinding and suffocating sandstorms, rain, mud, scorpions, lizards, and diseases, including boils, ague, typhus, malaria, and cholera.[3]

Abraham's journey was no easy one, especially when you add to the above problems the fact that the roads often harbored wandering troupes of bandits, and the whole political situation in the border region between what we know as Iraq and Turkey was no more stable in those days than it is as I write this a few months after the end of the U.S.-led war to oust Saddam Hussein from Iraq.

I have to confess that I'm chomping at the bit to make a trip to that part of the world myself—I'd love to try to retrace Abraham's footsteps. Frankly, however, I don't have the courage to put myself in that kind of a situation just yet. But Terah and Abraham did. Whether it was a journey of faith or merely the first faltering steps that would eventually lead to faith, they set out.

Is there something that scares you, but you sense you really ought to do it? Might it be something that will bring you closer to God and teach you to trust Him more? There have been many times like that in my own spiritual journey. Some of the steps have been scary.

How can we know whether the steps we're considering are mere folly? I think that as we continue our journey with Abraham, we'll notice that the main thing we have to do is to remain open to God's leading, wherever our journeys take us.

---

1. Jack Finegan, *Archaeological History of the Ancient Middle East* (New York: Dorset Press, 1979), 69.

2. A. Locher, *With Star and Crescent* (Philadelphia: Aetna Publishing Co., 1891), 307-310.

3. Katharine Eugenia Jones, "Backward Glance: Americans at Nippur," *Biblical Archaeology Review*, November/December 1998, 6.

CHAPTER FOUR

Detours

"The days of Terah were two hundred and five
years, and Terah died in Haran" (Genesis 11:32).

Terah and his family got as far as Haran and stopped. The fact that they ended up in that particular town gives us a pretty good idea what route they took. If they'd been taking the Euphrates River route to Canaan, they wouldn't have passed through Haran. That city is on the Balikh River, which flows into the Euphrates from the north. It's seventy miles from the Euphrates to Haran. That's almost a week of walking at caravan speed. If Terah really wanted to get to Canaan via the Euphrates route, a stop in Haran would seem to be out of the question.

The name *Haran* comes from the Akkadian word *Harannu,* which means "crossroads." Haran lay at the junction of two major trade routes, one running north and south, the other east and west. Today the site is in Turkey, just north of the Syrian border. Terah and company must have been traveling westward on the route that led from the Tigris River toward Syria and Palestine when they arrived in Haran.

By then, the old man may have been just plain worn out with travel. He and his family would have already logged at least 750 miles. A. Locher describes some of the terrain they would have passed through in the preceding month this way:

> The further we went towards our next halting place, Ernooz,
> the rougher and narrower became our path, so that before we reached

that village, the whole country, as far as the eye could reach, was a mass of rugged rocks studding densely the country around, and giving it the appearance of an ocean covered with petrified waves.

For miles and miles, the tortuous path was hardly discernible amidst the sea of rocks, and so narrow that it was nearly impossible for a quadruped the size of a cow or a horse to place a foot on real soil. . . .

After toiling painfully along over the outrageously uneven pavement of huge round boulders of extreme smoothness, with which the road at the entrance of the gorge is covered, we crossed the little brooklet that runs through this awe-inspiring gorge, and ignorantly struck into the wrong path, by swerving to our right, instead of the left, and soon found ourselves on very difficult and dangerous ground. However, we had to push on to the spot where the two paths rejoined each other, as there was no room to turn our horses round on the excessively narrow mountain path (hardly three feet wide), with a yawning precipice on one side and a bare, perpendicular rock on the other. Not a zephyr stirred the air, and the sun shone with relentless power upon our backs, as we slowly and cautiously climbed from ledge to ledge, leading our animals by the bridle.[1]

After enduring that kind of grueling travel for close to two months, who could blame a man of Terah's age for choosing to stop, at least for a little bit, when he reached the beautiful, well-watered valley of the Balikh.

In the year 1971 B.C., a well-educated and well-connected Egyptian by the name of Sinuhe found himself on the outs with the newly crowned Pharaoh, so he fled into exile. Upon his return to Egypt years later, he took the time to write an account of his life, and that account has survived. One of the places where he spent some time in the twentieth century B.C. was Haran. About it he wrote,

> It was a good land. Figs were in it, and grapes. It had more wine than water. Plentiful was its honey, abundant its olives. Every fruit was on its trees. Barley was there, and emmer [a hard, red wheat]. There was no limit to any cattle.[2]

JOURNEY TO MORIAH

Not only was it pleasant and fruitful, but it was also a great place to set up an import-export business—the very type of business the family had probably engaged in down in Ur. Haran already had a long history as a trading center. And Terah and company may have arrived at an especially opportune time. As I mentioned earlier, Mesopotamia had gone through a period of turmoil after the fall of the Third Dynasty of Ur. Many trade corridors had closed down. But things were starting to settle down by Terah's time, allowing caravans to travel more securely. Setting up business at a major crossroads could be a very wise business decision, allowing the family to get in on the ground floor of the reviving economy and make a lot of money.

Was this a detour on Terah's spiritual journey? If he'd set out for Canaan, would stopping short of that goal stunt his spiritual growth? Do we always have to keep pursuing the thing we first set out to do? Or is it safe to be flexible and acknowledge new opportunities as they present themselves?

SIDETRACKED IN HARAN?

If Terah's journey was indeed a spiritual quest, if he believed that God was leading him to new levels of closeness with Himself and that Canaan was the place to achieve that, then the stop in Haran had the potential to completely sidetrack his journey—because Haran was not only a great place for international commerce, it had always been an important religious center as well. It boasted the greatest temple to Ur's patron deity Nanna/Sin outside of downtown Ur. The question is—did this fact play a part in Terah's decision to stay? It's always nice, if you have to move, to settle down where you can associate with people of like faith, isn't it?

Some people may consider it heretical to suggest that Terah stopped in Haran because he felt comfortable in the local congregation of Nannaites. But remember, we have very little information about his motivation for moving in the first place. Nowhere does the Bible say that the Lord spoke to him and told him to move. He may have attributed to Nanna or some other god whatever spiritual impetus he responded to. Remember: Neither Abraham nor Terah knew the Lord by the name *Yahweh*, which was first revealed hundreds of years later to Moses (see Exodus 3:13-16; 6:3).

Could it be that Terah headed for Canaan sensing divine impetus or at least a restless urge to seek something better spiritually, but that when he arrived at Haran, weary from weeks of walking, some of the urgency had worn off? Old ways are comfortable ways—the more so the older we get. But going back to the old ways can become a detour if God was leading you to something better. When you set out to find a closer walk with God, it can be difficult to know which way to turn. It's possible to mistake coincidence or a good business opportunity for divine providence, isn't it? It's equally easy to get so enmeshed in day-to-day activities that we don't have the time to communicate with God and so miss out on the guidance He'd like to give us. Whether or not that's what happened to Terah and company, we do know that the march to Canaan stalled in Haran. It's impossible to know for exactly how long, because we don't know how old either Terah or Abraham was when they arrived there.

Genesis 11:26 says, "Terah lived seventy years, and begot Abraham, Nahor, and Haran." Taken very literally, this says that Terah's wife had triplets when Terah was seventy. But later we read that Terah lived until he was 205 years old (Genesis 11:32), and Genesis 12 implies that Abraham left Haran after Terah's death. If Abraham was born when Terah was seventy, then Abraham would have been at least 135 years old when he left Haran after his father's death. But Genesis 12:4 says he was only seventy-five. One way to solve this enigma is to assume that Abraham was born when Terah was 130, not seventy—in other words that Terah started having sons at age seventy, but Abraham was the kid brother, sixty years younger than the oldest. The fact that the year of Abraham's birth is left ambiguous in Genesis is just one more indication to me that the genealogies are included in the Bible for some reason other than to make it possible for us to calculate the age of the earth. I believe they are intended to point us to our heritage as sons and daughters of God and spiritual descendants of Abraham (see Galatians 3:29).

Please pardon the excursus. It was a bit of a detour in itself, but it's pertinent to the topic of spiritual journeys. I've watched too many Christians get bogged down obsessing over some tiny little detail. I read somewhere that a war was fought a few centuries ago between two Christian factions who couldn't agree on whether to make the sign of the cross with two fingers or three. I also read a news report in January 2000 that said that three men had been admitted to Goroka Base Hospital in Papua New Guinea with spear and arrow wounds. One man was in serious condition with head injuries. All of the injured were Baptists who had been fighting with some local Seventh-day Adventists about the prophetic importance of the year 2000. Somehow I sense that someone must have made a bit of a spiritual detour to arrive at the point where a question of the interpretation of prophecy had to be settled with spears and arrows.

Getting back to the story of Terah and Abraham, there's one additional possibility to consider regarding how long the whole troupe stayed in Haran. Genesis 11 seems to imply that Abraham stayed in Haran until his father died. That's the way I've always read the story. But it's just as possible to read the story and assume that it's simply saying that Haran is where Terah died, without linking his death to Abraham's departure at all. Perhaps Abraham left his aging father there, where he felt comfortable, and struck out on his own when he sensed God calling him to complete the journey to Canaan.

Whatever the case, Terah fades from the picture at this point. Spiritually dead or physically dead or just plain too old, too tired, or too distracted to pursue his quest any farther, he's no longer important to the story. Perhaps by getting his son pointed in the right direction he'd done all that God expected of him.

The focus of the story now turns to Abraham—because the younger man (he's only seventy-five!) has had something extraordinary happen to him. He's had an encounter with a god—an extraordinary encounter—in which the deity actually spoke to him. How will he respond to the voice of God? That's the question the rest of the story, and the rest of his journey, revolves around.

In fact, it's the question each and every one of us is challenged with every day. Am I caught on a detour? Has convenience or opportunity or fatigue halted my progress? If God wants to speak today—will I be ready to listen and follow?

---

1. A. Locher, *With Star and Crescent* (Philadelphia: Aetna Publishing, 1891), 435, 451, 452.
2. *Everyday Life in Bible Times* (Washington, D.C.: National Geographic Society, 1967), 75.

CHAPTER FIVE

Listening

"The LORD . . . said to Abram: 'Get out of your country, from your kindred and from your father's house, to a land that I will show you. I will make you a great nation; I will bless you and make your name great; and you shall be a blessing. I will bless those who bless you, and I will curse him who curses you; and in you all the families of the earth shall be blessed' " (Genesis 12:1-3).

How do you know when you're hearing the voice of God?

That can be a really tough question to answer. As a pastor, I've had occasion to counsel people who thought they were hearing God's voice telling them to do something that I didn't think God would tell them to do. How, for instance, do you convince a reclusively shy friend, who is so self-conscious that he covers his mouth with his hand when he speaks, that he shouldn't quit his current job and go to work selling Bibles door-to-door to support his family of four—especially when he thinks he hears God calling him to this line of work and other Christian leaders who don't know him as well as you do are telling him, "You can do it! Just trust God, and everything will work out fine."

Unfortunately, I never discovered the answer to that question. I told my friend that God gives us each certain spiritual gifts and that I felt he was gifted in other areas, but not for going out day after day to talk with strangers and persuade them to part with money for religious books. Still, he remained convinced that God was calling him, so he quit his janitorial job and went into sales. Within a few months he was in financial ruin, had withdrawn his children from church school, and had lost all faith in God and sworn off religion forever—a spiritual tragedy that I believe resulted from his mistaking his own ideas for the voice of God.

Remember the infamous New York serial killer David Berkowitz, also known as the Son of Sam? He heard what he thought was the voice of God telling him to kill one person after another. When people hear voices in their head telling them to do strange things, we say they're schizophrenics and give them medication to quiet their troubled soul.

I can hear the priest of Nanna at Haran asking Abraham, "What makes you so sure that it's your God talking to you? I mean, what you're planning to do is rather radical, isn't it? You say your God has told you to leave home—leave your whole family behind—and go off wandering until He tells you to stop? He's going to show you a land, or something, and when you get there, He's going to bless you and make your name great, and all the families of the earth will be blessed because of what you did?

"Abraham, let's think about this a little bit. In fact, let's do a little more praying about it before you do something rash. Have you ever heard of a condition called *megalomania,* in which a person has delusions of grandeur? They believe that somehow they've been called to fulfill some crucial role in the world, and if they fail, the whole world will be the worse off because of it. If you just sit back and relax a little, maybe it will go away.

"You say that all the families of earth are going to be blessed because of what you do. What about your own family? Look at your father here—he's a very old man. He'll soon be dying and going to the netherworld. It's your responsibility as a good son to bring the offerings to the temple for your father so that he can live well in the next world. If you travel off to some distant land, who will provide for him?"

Listening

There were all kinds of good reasons why Abraham shouldn't leave Haran. Good religious reasons: the gods down in Canaan where he figured he ought to go were all different. Good family reasons: family loyalties were extremely important to Mesopotamians. Sons usually didn't grow up, go off to college, meet a girl from another city, and move away. Families lived all together, taking over whole sections of cities, as is evidenced by archaeologists' discovery of large clusters of houses walled off from the rest of the city in ancient Nippur. Each compound where an extended family lived together was probably called a "father's house"—the very thing Abraham's God was telling him to leave (Genesis 12:1).

One of the many stories about the Sumerians' gods reveals a lot about marriage customs. When the god Dummuzi took Inanna for his wife, the newlyweds moved in with Inanna's parents for a short time. Then they moved to Dummuzi's family home, apparently to reside there on a permanent basis. That's where sons were supposed to stay—in their father's house.

Families intermarried among close relatives. Abraham himself was married to his half sister, a not-uncommon matrimonial arrangement no doubt decided upon by the parents. Such marriages helped keep the family wealth from being dispersed to outsiders. All the careful planning and intermarrying would have been in vain if one of the sons took off for parts unknown. It would be only natural for the family to cut off the inheritance of anyone who harbored such silly ideas.

And if you'd been raised in a city, the very thought of moving to the country—well, did you ever watch that old sitcom *Green Acres* with Eddie Albert and Eva Gabor? Mesopotamians' negative attitude toward the idea of moving to the country was far stronger than Eva's. To them, the city was the only place that was safe. Who knew what kind of demons might inhabit the lands around, where there was no ziggurat or temple to ensure the presence and happiness of the gods?

So, from a purely rational standpoint, the idea of leaving home and heading out for a place that your god would show you wouldn't stand up very well in a family council meeting.

JOURNEY TO MORIAH

A PERSONAL GOD

However, to acquire a personal god who would actually communicate with you—that seemed like a good thing, a very lucky thing. In fact, in both Akkadian and Sumerian—the two major languages of ancient Mesopotamia—the only way to describe good luck or good fortune was to say the lucky person had "acquired a god." In omen texts, written by priests or prophets who claimed to be able to see the future, to tell a family that their house would "acquire a god," was about the best news a prophet could deliver. Conversely, when a priest or prophet predicted, "That house will not acquire a god, that house will not endure,"[1] it was bad news indeed!

"So, Abraham, you're pretty sure you've acquired a personal god who is interested in blessing your house and making it endure, are you?" I can hear Terah saying to his son.

"Yes I am, Dad," Abraham responds.

"But you've been married more than forty years and don't even have any children yet."

"I know, Dad. That's part of why it's so important to me to follow the leading of this God. He's promised me lots of descendants."

"I see. Well, that seems like a good thing. We've been worried about Sarah's barrenness, you know. But I suppose that means that your God will lead you to a different wife in this new land.

"What about inheritances? We've worked very hard to build up the family fortune. All our marriages have been carefully planned to guard against losses—"

"I know, Dad. I've thought about all that. And you know what? It really doesn't matter to me. I'm so sure about this—well, it just doesn't matter. You can cut me off from the family inheritance if you want; that way there won't be any risk to you. I'll just take Sarah and my personal servants and the things I can claim as my own. You and Mom and Nahor and the rest of the family can stay here in Haran and keep the business going. Don't worry—you'll hear from us after we get settled in the new land that God shows me. You'll hear how my God has blessed us there. Maybe we can even set up a new trading outpost down there and send caravans back and forth!"

Listening

Terah sees a bit of himself in his son—wanderlust, a thirst for adventure. How can he, who has led his family so far from home, argue with Abraham's ambitions? Hadn't they been his own ambitions to start with? Didn't he remember something about setting out to go to Canaan? Perhaps that is where this God is leading his son. Perhaps what he is hearing is merely a continuation—or fulfillment—of his own dream.

Terah stares long and hard at his well-worn sandals and the dust they rest in. He had hoped to have descendants as numerous as the specks of dust on the earth. But the death of one son in Ur and the fruitless marriage he'd arranged for Abraham had put a bit of a crimp on those expectations. Maybe it could still happen. Maybe his house had acquired a god at long last. Maybe it would endure.

He looks up at his son. "This god—what did you say his name is? Perhaps we should consult with the priests and soothsayers to find out if he is a powerful god or not."

"He didn't tell me His name yet, Dad. But I'm pretty sure He's the same God that our ancestors worshiped many generations ago—back in the days of Noah."

"I see. If that's so, He is an exceedingly powerful God. It would be a good thing if our family could acquire such a powerful deity for our own." Terah breaks off for a moment and looks at the dust again, then looks up at his beloved son. "I hope you're right about this."

"Then I have your blessing?" Abraham asks.

"You have my blessing," his father replies. "But as to the family's wealth—that will have to be worked out in a council of the elders."

Did Abraham wait until after his father had died to break away from his family? We don't know for sure. But even if he didn't, he can't have had any serious expectation of ever seeing his father again when he departed. God was calling him to go somewhere else. And later aspects of the story demonstrate that Abraham's decision to follow that call meant he could never look back. Could never go back. Maybe the family council told him as much: "If you leave, don't you ever come crying back here, looking for a handout!" one of the men may have shouted in frustration. And Abraham may have responded, "Don't worry—you won't be seeing me around here ever again. I'd rather starve to death!"

JOURNEY TO MORIAH

Or the parting may have been more amicable. In either case, it was permanent. If Terah wasn't dead, he might as well have been, because Abraham wouldn't be seeing him again.

When I first began this manuscript, my own mother was near death. I often found myself angry without reason. I began to look at both the past and future through different eyes. Mother always was the treasure trove of memories in our family, remembering names, dates, and details about events that the rest of us could only vaguely reconstruct. Along with being our link with the past, she was an important bridge to my future. I wanted never to disappoint her—I wanted always to make her proud. Partly for her sake I walked a circumspect path through life. With her death impending I found one of the supports beneath my bridge to the future gone, and I began to wonder in ways I seldom had before about what lay ahead.

Breaking the bonds of home and family must have had a similar effect on Abraham. When you live in a patriarchal family, a lot of your decisions are made for you. As Abraham and Sarah, along with Lot, Abraham's nephew (who perhaps decided to go along for adventure or just to see how things turned out), and a few others headed west out of Haran, a great sense of responsibility descended on Abraham. But he, and the rest of his caravan, must have felt a lot of anticipation too.

They must have wondered when he would next hear from his God, for instance. Would a voice suddenly speak from the sky and say, "Company, halt—one, two!" And could they then unload the donkeys, set up camp, and claim the territory for their descendants in perpetuity? And how far would they have to go? Two days' journey? Three? A week or two?

IMPRESSED BY EBLA

If Abraham had any hope that this part of his spiritual journey would be a quick, easy jaunt, he was in for a disappointment. Four days of walking probably brought the family to the next major town, Carchemish, where they could cross the Euphrates and head south. The next stopping place that we hear about after Abraham left Haran is Shechem in Canaan. But the distance between those two points is about 550 miles by the route I think the family took.

What would they have encountered along the way? Vast, wide-open spaces where they could easily stop and claim a piece of the future? Well, yes, there were no doubt long stretches of uninhabited territory along the trail. But it was all land that somebody claimed. There were small kingdoms centered in places like Alalalakh, Aleppo, Emar, Ebla, Hamath, and Qatna. At that time, the borders between these various city-states probably weren't particularly stable. But still, they claimed the land.

Of the cities Abraham must have passed, the most important would have been Ebla, which has been carefully excavated by teams from the University of Rome over the past forty years. It had recently undergone some massive reconstruction when Abraham passed by and was nearly restored to the glory it had displayed three centuries earlier, before it was destroyed by King Naram-Sin of the old Akkadian Empire.

Situated on top of a hill, with powerfully constructed earthen walls that still stand more than sixty-five feet high in some places, the city of thirty thousand souls would have made quite an impression on travelers. If Abraham and company paused long enough to go into the city for provisions, they would have had to pass under the watchful eye of guards stationed in a watchtower and then through a heavily fortified gateway that forced those entering the city to go around a gradual forty-five degree curve, then face a second, more massive gatehouse that had large rooms where defending soldiers could mass to waylay any enemy who had made it past the first gate. The architecture of such cities was designed to create awe and fear in the hearts of any who might be tempted to think of attacking.

Inside the city, Abraham could have visited at least three temples, one of which was dedicated to Ishtar—a rough equivalent of Inanna, with whom he would have been acquainted in Ur. A smaller temple was dedicated to Resheph, the Canaanite god of war, and a third to the sun god, who was called Shamash here, rather than Utu. Other gods worshiped in Ebla included Baal, Malik, Kura, Adad, and the most important of the Canaanite gods, El. Since El was the father of the other gods in the Canaanite pantheon, his name came to mean "god" in a generic sense. When the Lord identified Himself to Abraham, He used the name El in this general sense, but added an adjective that revealed some particular characteristic. El Elyon means "God Most High." El Shaddai is usually translated "God Almighty." After God helped Hagar in the wilderness, she referred to Him as El Roi—"the God who sees."

Finding a city like Ebla—of comparable size to his native Ur—in the land to which he was journeying must have given Abraham pause to think about the journey he was making. Upon returning to the land years later, some of his descendants would look around and bring back a report that there were "giants in the land," inspiring fear rather than faith in the hearts of those to whom God had promised the land. But Abraham kept on journeying, looking around at what he saw, pondering God's purpose for his life, waiting to hear God say "Stop."

Ebla was less than two hundred miles into his journey. Another two hundred miles brought him to Damascus, and he must have stopped there, because later in the story, in Genesis 15, we hear of one Eliezer of Damascus, whom Abraham calls his heir. That little comment about Eliezer's status gives us some clues to details of the story that aren't obvious until you start reading between the lines.

The great biblical archaeologist William Foxwell Albright has suggested, based on ancient documents discovered in the Middle East, that there's a good reason why a servant from Damascus would be Abraham's legal heir. It seems that Damascus was a major banking center. And because banks didn't have branch offices in every village and town in those days, they had to devise alternate means for seeing to it that their business was properly attended to in distant lands. If a foreigner came to them looking for a loan—perhaps to cover expenses for a caravan or some other business—they'd ante up the cash. But they'd also see to it that their money would find its way home again by attaching one major stipulation: They'd require that the borrower take one of their staff members along on his journey to keep track of the money. Better yet, if it was a major loan, they'd require the borrower to adopt someone from their town as legal heir. That way there'd be no way around paying back the loan—with interest. Even if the borrower died along the way, his adopted son—the bank staffer from Damascus—would inherit the cash and bring it back home.

So, when Genesis 15 introduces us to Eliezer, it clues us in to some pertinent details about Abraham's life. By time Abraham got to Damascus, he must have needed a loan. The relatives up north must have cut him off from the family business resources.

This detail also reveals something about Abraham's character: He's a resourceful man; a businessman who knows the ropes. He may be a man of faith, but he's not going to just sit around praying about things and hoping problems will solve themselves. He takes matters in hand and does what needs to be done. While journeying along and listening for the voice of God, he doesn't turn off his own mind or take a "God will provide, so why should I worry" attitude. Later in the story, God has to labor with him on this point, to help him get the balance between self-dependence and God-dependence right.

Knowing just how to strike the proper balance between leaving things in God's care and doing what we need to do on our own is a challenge for all of us who believe in God. But as we continue journeying with Abraham, listening for the voice of God, He will teach us.

---

1. Thorkild Jacobsen, *The Treasures of Darkness* (New Haven: Yale University Press, 1976), 155.

CHAPTER SIX

Wandering

"Abram passed through the land to the place of Shechem, as far as the terebinth tree of Moreh. And the Canaanites were then in the land" (Genesis 12:6).

I opened chapter five with the question "How do you know when you're hearing the voice of God?" but I never really answered it, did I? We can look at Abraham's experience—with four millennia of hindsight to our advantage—and say, "Yes, it was God's voice he heard. It's a good thing he listened and followed its leading." But the question remains: How can we know—without the benefit of hindsight—that the voice we hear is God's?

I've always answered that question by pointing out that today we have the benefit of thousands of years' worth of recorded experiences of those who listened to God. We have the Bible—all sixty-six books of it—to go to for case histories. When in doubt, we can turn to this record of God's leading people through the years and compare. If what we're hearing doesn't jibe with what's in the Bible, we have good reason to question whether the voice is really God's. But Abraham didn't have the Bible to rely on.

After leaving Damascus, Abraham probably traveled down the major trade route known as the King's Highway, which skirted the western edge of the Arabian Desert, until he was a little southeast of Shechem. A few miles south of the Jabbok River there was a road that ran west-

Wandering

ward down into the Jordan Valley. It forded the Jordan at Adamah and continued up the Wadi Faria, crossing the central hills of Canaan between Mt. Gilboa and Mt. Ebal at Shechem. In those days this must have been the preferred route to Canaan from points north, because it's the route Jacob chose for his return trip from Haran about two centuries later (see Genesis 32:22; 33:17, 18). A modern traveler describes the area Abraham and Lot passed through in the Jordan Valley like this:

> This area, irrigated by the Jabbok's waters, blooms in fragrant fertility, made all the more pleasant by contrast with the gaunt bareness of the hillsides above it. Dominating the rich bottomland is a small mound whose modern name, Tell Damieh, reflects the Biblical name of Adamah.[1]

The thought of staying in such a pleasant place must have been tempting. But the voice of God was not here. Nothing that said, "This is the place." No command to halt. So the intrepid travelers moved on. But Lot tucked a memory of the spot into the back of his mind.

As Abraham journeyed from place to place, he passed through many convenient locales where he could have stopped and established residence, as his father had done at Haran. He also met all kinds of people with all kinds of opinions about what the gods wanted and how to make contact with the gods. So he had to stay closely attuned to the voice he had heard in the first place.

Did he do that at Shechem? Let's look at the story again:

> Abram traveled through the land until he came to the sacred tree of Moreh, the holy place at Shechem. (At that time the Canaanites were still living in the land.) The LORD appeared to Abram and said to him, "This is the country that I am going to give to your descendants." Then Abram built an altar there to the LORD, who had appeared to him. After that, he moved on south to the hill country east of the city of Bethel and set up his camp between Bethel on the west and Ai on the east. There also he built an altar and worshiped the LORD (Genesis 12:6-8, TEV).

JOURNEY TO MORIAH

I chose to quote the above verses from Today's English Version because the translators picked up on one of the subtleties of the Hebrew. Most versions ignore it, calling the spot where Abraham stopped merely "the place of Shechem" (NKJV, for instance). The TEV calls it "the holy place at Shechem" because the Hebrew word *maqom* often refers to a special place of worship. It stands to reason that if Abraham was going to choose a place at which to listen for God's voice, he'd select a location that the locals thought was a good spot to make contact with the divine.

Even the tree where he stopped seems to have special significance for a spiritual pilgrim. The TEV calls it the "sacred tree of Moreh." Hebrew scholars give it titles such as "the Oracular Oak" or "the tree of the oracle-giver."[2] In a later story about Shechem, the New King James Version refers to "the Diviner's Terebinth Tree" (Judges 9:37). Abraham seems to have had a special interest in trees like this, because later he spends a lot of time by the "terebinth trees of Mamre." The Hebrew word used to describe these trees is the same one used of the tree at Shechem. You may also recall that the prophetess Deborah, sat under a special tree to answer the questions of people who came to her for advice (see Judges 4:5).

THE SONS OF A DONKEY

Shechem apparently had a long history as a place of worship and a place for entering into a special relationship with God. It's interesting that when Jacob arrived there, the inhabitants were known as "the children of Hamor"—literally the sons of a donkey (see Genesis 33:19). About that time a large temple stood there as well. It was known as the temple of El-Berith—the temple of the God of the covenant. Significantly, documents found in nearby cities reveal that a foal of a donkey was often sacrificed as part of the ceremony involved in establishing a covenant between two groups of people. So, the sons of Hamor may have been a clan that specialized in providing donkeys to groups of people who were establishing covenant-based relationships. And the god worshiped by the Canaanites at Shechem must have been a god who specialized in solemnizing human relationships.

Wandering

Abraham wouldn't have had to know all the details. He'd probably just heard that Shechem had a suitable place for making contact with his God again. It seems as though he hadn't received any messages from God during his five-hundred-plus-mile journey. Abraham no doubt worshiped, prayed, and listened, but there's no record that God responded with any more than the usual general sense of acceptance one receives from such religious exercises. It's as though once God got Abraham headed in the right direction, He just let him keep marching, waiting till he got to the right place before giving any further instructions.

That seems to fit well with the original arrangements between the man and his God. "You go.... I'll show," God says in Genesis 12:1, and there doesn't seem to be any reason to expect the "I'll show" part until the man has arrived in the right place.

Does God sometimes work that way in your life too? Do you ever find yourself going for days, perhaps weeks, without any sense of special revelation or special closeness with God? You can't see any sign that you've strayed from the path He wants you on, but you just kind of run on spiritual autopilot for a while. There's nothing wrong with that, as along as you stay tuned in, ready to hear when God speaks and ready to act on what you hear.

So, is that what Abraham did at Shechem? Read the account carefully:

The LORD appeared to Abram and said to him, "This is the country that I am going to give to your descendants." Then Abram built an altar there to the LORD, who had appeared to him. After that, he moved on south" (Genesis 12:7, 8, TEV).

What, exactly, was it that Abraham was waiting to hear from the Lord? Would "this is the country"—"this is the place"—be a likely line to listen for, do you think?

It sounds good to me. In fact, the thing I expect to read next about Abraham is that he unloaded the donkeys, unpacked the tents, put the sheep out to pasture, and set up camp. I mean, he's walked more than five hundred miles. If I were he, I think all I'd need to hear is "this is the place" and I'd never say "Head 'em up move 'em out" again! I'd be there to stay.

JOURNEY TO MORIAH

But what did Abraham do? He built an altar. Not that there wasn't already an altar there, but he took the time to build his own. This was his special place—the place where God first *appeared* to him. If you've got a highlighter nearby, highlight that word *appeared* right now because it's very important throughout the story. The God who *appears* and the God who *sees* are core elements of Abraham's spiritual journey. Whenever the idea of seeing or appearing occurs in the story, it involves the same Hebrew root word, which can be translated "see" or "provide." That little play on words will be a crucial part of Abraham's learning process as he moves toward his final examination on Mt. Moriah.

People might have worshiped other gods there at Shechem. They might have built other altars for establishing covenants between peoples who met there. But Abraham wanted no part of that. He built his own altar, prepared his own sacrifice, and called on the name of his personal God.

What a wonderful thing: to go all that way in hope of meeting your God, and then to arrive and find Him there waiting for you—in visible form! It would give you a real warm, fuzzy feeling, wouldn't it? You'd say, "This is an awesome place," wouldn't you? You'd never want to leave, would you?

So what did Abraham do? He built an altar *and moved on!*

What went wrong? Why didn't he stay in Shechem, if that's where God appeared to him and announced that this was the place He intended to give to his descendants?

The story offers only one clue, one little sentence: "The Canaanites were then in the land." Abraham must have looked around and said, "Hmmm. This can't be the right place. There are people living here already. I thought God was going to give me some free land."

There was another factor too, though. Abraham was a flatlander. From Ur you can see to the horizon in almost any direction without so much as a hummock in view. Haran is surrounded by mountains, but the city is in a valley, with a river to water your livestock, and plenty of flat pasture land.

The area around Shechem, on the other hand, is rocky and hilly, and much of it was covered with forests. I've been to Shechem only once, at the end of a long hot summer, and the area looked pretty dry and barren. But Shechem actually receives more rainfall in an average year than does San Francisco. There's good evidence that the central mountains of Palestine once had extensive areas of forest, just as the hills around San Francisco do, and that at least a few areas were suitable for flocks of sheep, cattle, and goats to graze.

Precisely because of its inhospitableness, the area wasn't heavily settled when Abraham arrived. Still, to adapt to living in an area so different from home would require a major learning curve. Maybe Abraham and company stayed for a while but found it just too difficult to make the adjustment and decided to move on.

When you set out to follow the Lord, it's possible to fall into a rut, to let your spiritual journey become more of a habit than an adventure. To just keep on keeping on with the same old same old. And to miss God's ideal plan for you because you thought you ought to keep doing what you've always done instead of accepting the challenge of doing things a new way, learning new things, and developing new skills. Real, growing faith often gets challenged and shaken up—asked to do things it hasn't had to do before. That's not a bad thing, because it helps keep us fresh. And it makes us keep relying on God to supply what we need instead of just going on in our own wisdom and strength.

Personally, I think that's what God had planned for Abraham at Shechem. But Abraham missed the call. He must have decided God wasn't really serious about *this* being the *exact* place. Someplace else would do just as well, wouldn't it?

Terah hit a detour when he stopped too soon. Abraham hit one when he didn't stop soon enough. And at that point he began to try to lead God instead of letting himself be led.

That's a sure way to hit a detour. But Abraham didn't seem to realize it, and so he wandered on.

---

1. Nelson Glueck, *The River Jordan* (Philadelphia: The Jewish Publication Society of America, 1946), 143.

2. See for instance Lawrence E. Stager's translation in *Biblical Archaeology Review,* July/August 2003, 34, and Claus Westermann's comments in *Genesis 12-36,* John J. Scullion, trans., (Minneapolis: Fortress Press, 1985), 153, 154.

CHAPTER SEVEN

Searching

"He moved from there to the mountain east of Bethel, and he pitched his tent with Bethel on the west and Ai on the east; there he built an altar to the LORD and called on the name of the LORD. So Abram journeyed, going on still toward the South. Now there was a famine in the land, and Abram went down to Egypt to sojourn there, for the famine was severe in the land" (Genesis 12:8-10).

How does God respond to spiritual pilgrims who miss their cues?

It probably took Abraham and company a couple days to get from Shechem to Bethel. And it wouldn't have been easy walking. Almost all of it was either uphill or downhill along the spine of Canaan—the central mountain range.

Perhaps by the time he got to Bethel, Abraham had begun to wonder if he'd done the right thing. What about it? He had met his God back there at Shechem. Had he left Him behind now? Better stop and do a communication check.

Such a check is not a bad idea when you begin to wonder if you're running ahead of God on your spiritual journey. Time for a spiritual retreat, perhaps. Or a trip to camp meeting. Or maybe just a good long hike in the woods. Whatever you choose, you need to make it a time when you pause from your busyness trying to do God's work (or your own work) and focus on your relationship with God. And, especially, you need to make it a time to listen for God's voice. To make sure you haven't gotten off the track.

When I was about thirteen, my dad and I took a trip up into the mountains of Oregon. I'll always remember it—it was definitely one of the highlights of my growing-up years. We loaded the family tent and our fishing poles into the old Ford Fairlane, and off we went to explore territory where we'd never been before.

By noon we'd reached the top of the mountains at a place called Summit Lake. We got out the fishing poles but soon discovered that the only thing biting was mosquitoes. That was OK with me though, because I was more interested in exploring the forest than catching fish anyhow. So I left Dad sitting by the lake and went on a journey of discovery.

After climbing up a hill, I turned around and went down to the bottom—only to discover that I'd gotten on the wrong side of the hill, and neither the lake nor my dad was anywhere to be seen. Seemed like a simple problem to solve, so I climbed back up near the top of the hill again and went down a different side.

Still no lake and no dad.

After a third trip to the top and back down, I began to feel lost. I hurried back up the hill, my heart beating faster than it needed to. This time when I got near the top I tried a new strategy.

"Hello!" I called as loudly as I could. I called again, and a third time. Then I heard a faint "Hello" in return, at about a thirty-degree angle from where I thought Dad ought to be. "Just keep calling," I shouted. "I want to follow your voice."

And follow his voice I did—all the way to the lake and safety.

I'm glad that I had the good sense to stop and call to him instead of just beating my way through the bush in search of the elusive lake. Abraham seems to have had that kind of good sense too. After a couple days of sandal-pounding the paths of Palestine, he stopped, climbed to the top of a hill, looked around, and called out to God.

But he got no answer. No one called back a reassuring "Hello!" God didn't say, "Yes! I'm right over here! Just follow My voice, and everything will be all right."

JOURNEY TO MORIAH

When I was a young pastor, I met a big burly fellow named Neal. He attended my church a few times but then got discouraged and quit coming. I stopped by his home to visit him, and the better I got to know him, the more I liked him.

Eventually, I asked him what it would take to get him back on the path with God. He sat quietly for a moment, then raised his big, work-ingman hand and pointed his index finger at the chair across the room from him. "I want God to come down here and sit in that chair and talk to me. Then I'll believe in Him," he said.

Is it our right to make demands like that of God?

Isn't that about what Abraham did, by building an altar two dozen miles south of where God had appeared to him?

What should we expect when we demand that God follow us instead of vice versa?

MY PRAYER AS AN ATHEIST

I'm not sure what Abraham expected, but what he got was silence. So did Neal. As for me, there was a time when I was an atheist. I'd written God completely off as an invention of humankind's wishful thinking. I'd quit praying, abandoned the Bible, and basically tuned religion out of my life. Then one day I prayed almost accidentally. I didn't even say it out loud; I just let a thought run through my mind: *God, if you're really out there—solve this problem for me!* And the next day the problem got solved in a most remarkable way that pointed me back to God and transformed my life.

Why does God sometimes hear whispers and other times ignore shouts? I don't claim to be God, so I don't claim to have the answer to that question. But if there's one thing we can learn from this part of Abraham's story, it's that even when we get off the path and can't seem to find the way back to where we last met God, He doesn't abandon us. He may exercise a little tough love by letting us go our own way for a while. But if He sees in our hearts a fundamental openness to hearing His voice, He'll keep His eye on us. Watching from afar, maybe. Keeping quiet in the shadows. Waiting for the right moment to intervene again and set us back on the right path.

Searching

God let Abraham go all the way to Egypt. There was a famine in the land, and the farther Abraham went, the drier things got. But he kept on going. It seems never to have occurred to him to turn around and go back to Shechem. Maybe that would have seemed too much like surrender. Too much like backtracking. Maybe it would be too tempting—once he headed north—to just keep on going and not stop until he reached Haran. And that wouldn't be a good thing. He'd said he'd never be back, and he'd never before eaten crow. Why start at this age?

So he kept going. Past Salem (Jerusalem). Past Hebron. Past Beersheba. Through desert wastelands few would want to cross in a Humvee, let alone on foot. It must have been a punishing journey. And by the time the weary travelers reached the line of forts the Twelfth Dynasty pharaohs had erected to keep the nomads they called "sand crossers" from encroaching on their kingdom, the travelers' financial, physical, and spiritual resources must have been severely depleted.

I can picture Abraham one night well into the journey sitting beside the cooking fire swapping stories with other men—perhaps longhaul drivers he'd met at a donkey stop on the King's Highway. At times like that, the talk often turns to the type of people you're likely to meet at various places. Stories start to fly across the fire—stories about atrocities, injustices, cruelties. City rulers who steal slaves, children, even wives. Men who've been killed while trying to defend their families. "But you know what's the worst place of all?" a scar-faced man asks, his half-grin revealing a mouth missing most of its teeth.

"Egypt!" a chorus of voices shouts in unison around the fire—all agreeing that the nation to the south has the roughest reputation of all for making unreasonable demands on travelers.

Abraham is in the thick of the conversation at first, sharing his own tales, even telling about his quest to find God. But as the stories grow more vivid and coarse, he falls silent and simply listens. By the time he slips away to bed, the roast lamb he had for dinner is kicking up its heels in his stomach. He spends a rough night, tossing and turning, dreaming of cruelties he may face on the trail. He awakes in the morning with a plan in mind. A simple little thing that just might save his skin.

"Sarah," he says to his wife, who's been up for an hour already, preparing barley loaves for breakfast. "Such tales I heard last night around the fire."

"Yes, I heard them too," she replies.

"Fearful things. . . . I didn't sleep well."

"Nor did I."

"What will happen to us if we meet some of these cruel men?"

"Well, we're not going to Egypt, are we?"

"I suppose not."

"Then perhaps we won't meet such cruel men."

"Perhaps not," Abraham says and walks away, his head hanging, to check on the men tending his flocks. As he walks, he looks around at all that he owns—every cent he ever had is wrapped up in these sheep, cattle, donkeys, camels, and the servants who tend them. It could all be taken away so easily. And for the first time he begins to think about just how vulnerable he is—a man without a country. A man with no family nearby to avenge him should he fall prey to some scam or coercion.

Yes, he decides, he must plan ahead. Make provision for every exigency. "Sarah," he says when he returns to the cooking fire, "this is what you must do if we come up against a situation like those we heard about last night. We are brother and sister. Children of the same father. If the men of the place ask, you must say of me, 'He's my brother.' Understand?" (see Genesis 20:13).

Whether she understood or not, it was not Sarah's right, in that society, to question her husband or disagree. And she didn't. So it was all arranged. Without ever planning to go to Egypt, Abraham had already decided what cowardly course he would take if he got there.

We all have our price, it's said. A point where we'll sacrifice integrity for survival, or maybe just for profit. If we intentionally set that point beforehand, it's almost guaranteed we'll arrive at it someday.

Abraham did.

CHAPTER EIGHT

Salvation

> "So it was, when Abram came into Egypt, that the
> Egyptians saw the woman, that she was very
> beautiful. The princes of Pharaoh also saw her and
> commended her to Pharaoh. And the woman was
> taken to Pharaoh's house. He treated Abram well
> for her sake. He had sheep, oxen, male donkeys,
> male and female servants, female donkeys, and
> camels" (Genesis 12:14-16).

By the time he arrived in Egypt, Abraham must have been tired—physically, emotionally, and spiritually. And the devil must have been waiting for him at the border.

Egypt held at least nominal control of much of Canaan at this time. Some scholars think the pharaohs probably administered the territory through local rulers stationed at places like Shechem, Byblos, Beth Shan, and Jerusalem. Just how effective the control was is subject to dispute. Execration texts found by archaeologists in Egypt give us a clue that the rulers may have been grasping at straws to maintain their hold—hoping that magic spells would do the trick.

An execration text is a curse or spell written against an enemy. The Egyptians in Abraham's day would write these texts on clay pots and statues, then smash them and bury them in a holy place. They hoped that doing this would make the curse effective. The process probably didn't help the Egyptians a whole lot, but it has been a windfall for modern archaeologists, because they've picked up the broken pieces and put them back together again to discover which areas the Egyptians were concerned with at that time. Place names occurring on these broken bits of clay that are of interest to Bible readers include Jerusalem, Ashkelon, Beth Shan, Aphek, and Tyre.

From this era also we have the story of Sinuhe, the official who fled from Egypt to Canaan under a cloud of suspicion. The fact that he had to go as far as Byblos and then inland from there to feel safe from Egyptian agents is another indication of the breadth of the pharaohs' power during Abraham's life.

So, before our patriarch friend ever approached the border, he must have been reasonably well acquainted with Egyptian power. No wonder he was worried about what would happen to him on account of Sarah.

Just here there's something I personally struggle with in the story. By this time, according to Genesis 12, Abraham is at least seventy-five years old. We know Sarah was just ten years younger than he (Genesis 17:17), so she's no spring chicken either. Twenty-four or twenty-five years later, we get a similar story about Abraham and Sarah at Gerar (Genesis 20), well after Sarah has passed childbearing age. The natural question to ask is, Why would kings be stealing old women, far past their prime? Marriage age in this culture was probably more like twelve or fifteen for women. So I can't help but wonder whether Abraham and Sarah were really as old as the text says they were when they set out on their journey. The events just don't seem to jibe with the stated ages. And I'm more inclined to think that the story is true and the age got mixed up somewhere than to abandon the story as false because it seems so odd that a king would bother to steal a woman who was sixty-five or ninety years old on account of her beauty or her potential as a child bearer.

Maybe questions like that don't bother you when you read the Bible, but they do me. I want to know what really happened. So when two aspects of a story don't fit together, I recognize that I have to choose between the two or else rationalize in some way that involves more of a leap of faith than I think God expects us to take. I think that throwing out all rational questions about genuine anomalies in the Bible and saying "God said it; I believe it; that settles it for me" ultimately weakens our faith because it separates faith from reason. And God does say, "Come, let us reason together," doesn't He?

Some people, seeing what they consider to be inconsistencies or contradictions in the Bible, use them as an excuse for abandoning all faith in God—which to me makes about as much sense as finding an error in the current issue of the *New England Journal of Medicine* and abandoning all faith in doctors and medication.

These kinds of questions are important to some people, so we can't just ignore them. If we want to be able to talk intelligently with a genuine seeker from a secular background who wonders about this type of problem in the Bible, we can't just demand of that person that he or she accept that postmenopausal Sarah was still so attractive at age ninety that men would kill for her. With such a person I'd rather concede that maybe the numbers or the exact dates when things happened aren't totally accurate than concede that maybe the story is made up out of whole cloth. I'm not sure that the kind of flexibility in accepting dates I've described is my final answer on how to deal with perceived anomalies in the Bible. I'm still learning, and plan to keep learning until the day I die. Having said all this, we'll continue to take the ages listed in the Bible as the basis of interpreting the story, because they're part of the story.

Are you comfortable having loose ends in your walk with God? Or does everything have to be sewed up tight, with no unanswered questions? Notice that when Abraham didn't think things were quite right, he didn't turn his back on God or intentionally run away from Him. He kept experimenting in his relationship to divinity. "OK," he said, "it doesn't seem to be working well for us here—let's move down the road a couple days' journey, and see what happens there." And he just kept on moving. Not abandoning his faith—just being what you might call an experimental believer. Nonetheless, the farther he got from the place he'd last seen God, the more his faith suffered. I don't think he abandoned it. It just got buried under the other layers of his life. And he went back to his "normal" self—relying more on his wits than on faith to guide him.

For me, the most encouraging thing is that God didn't abandon Abraham while he was working these things out—even though Abraham really blew it in the matter of Sarah and Pharaoh. I mean *really* blew it.

JOURNEY TO MORIAH

ABRAHAM SACRIFICES HIS WIFE

The main dwelling place of the kings of Egypt at this time was quite a ways up the Nile—twenty or thirty miles past modern Cairo and the pyramids of Giza. But the royals also had a palace down in the Nile delta, probably in about the area where Jacob and his sons moved years later. So it seems unlikely that Abraham and company went all the way up to the capital city.

Here's what did happen, though:

> It came to pass, when he was close to entering Egypt, that he said to Sarai his wife, "Indeed I know that you are a woman of beautiful countenance. Therefore it will happen, when the Egyptians see you, that they will say, 'This is his wife'; and they will kill me, but they will let you live. Please say you are my sister, that it may be well with me for your sake, and that I may live because of you" (Genesis 12:11-13).

Put in the plainest terms, Abraham was willing to sacrifice his wife to save himself. Sarah was to be the sacrificial lamb laid on the altar to preserve the life of the patriarch. He still had a lot of learning to do about who his real Savior was. But for the time being, Sarah would serve as an adequate substitute.

Did she go willingly? Was she tired of following this vagabond husband who claimed to have special revelations from God? Would finally getting to settle down in a real house—even if it was just a harem—actually seem like a treat after all this uncertainty? Maybe so. But I can hardly believe that she looked forward with relish to being the bedtime toy of a megalomaniac who thought he was a god.

And what about Abraham? What was he thinking? Was there nothing else he could give to the Egyptians to satisfy their greed? Genesis 12:5 seems to indicate that when he left Haran he had plenty of the world's goods to take with him. And verse 16 describes his wealth after he surrendered Sarah to Pharaoh—almost as though we should be surprised that the man has all these things again. As though he'd lost most of his worldly possessions on the way to Egypt, and only by giving

Sarah to Pharaoh did he become a wealthy man again. He obviously got a handsome bride price for his sister/wife.

But would all those things assuage his conscience? Could they replace the woman who had followed him so faithfully for so far, not even questioning his egregiously self-serving ways when he sent her away? Would it be hard for him to get used to life without Sarah? Did he perhaps rationalize that he was doing her a favor? Or was it himself he was doing a favor? Was he a scheming man, looking for ways to help God keep His promises?

Sarah was, after all, infertile. That was an obvious fact of life. Hadn't God promised him descendants? The promise had been to him, not to Sarah. So he had God's word on the fact that he was able to make babies. He'd been trying with Sarah for years, so maybe it was time to try "plowing another field."

Whatever they taught kids in sex-ed classes in southern Mesopotamia four thousand years ago, it didn't have much to do with what we understand about human reproduction today. The average fourth-grader today probably knows more about how babies are made than Abraham did. The ancient Mesopotamian languages had no special word to describe semen. They simply called it water, and it fit into their scheme of things the same way the spring rains and the rising of the rivers did. When water hit the soil, life sprang up. In the marriage relationship, the man was like the water god Enki—supplying the life-engendering fluid. But the woman needed to be fertile soil for the combination to yield fruit.

In other words, there was no possibility that a man might be infertile. As long as he could produce the necessary fluid, he had done his part. It was the woman's responsibility to respond to the fluid by sprouting new life. If she didn't, then she was the one who was infertile.

So, maybe turning Sarah over to Pharaoh wasn't such a bad thing after all. She would have a decent future under the care of a king, which was better than Abraham could promise her. It probably had occurred to him before this opportunity presented itself that he ought to be looking for another wife anyway. Mesopotamian customs allowed a man to have two wives, but in his pre-Egypt financial straits, he might have found it hard to support more than one. So, yes, send Sarah off to

Pharaoh (without mentioning that she was infertile, of course), collect the bride price, and *voilà!* you've solved two problems at once. Brilliant!

See how easy it is to rationalize when you're on a spiritual journey and you've wandered away from God and begun to rely on your wits instead of your faith? It's amazing isn't it, the things we can come up with to justify bad behavior. But what's even more amazing is the length to which God will go to rescue us from ourselves.

In a foretaste of what would happen to the pharaohs of a much later dynasty who took away all the sons of Jacob's descendants, the pharaoh who took Sarah away suddenly began to feel the hand of God resting heavily on him. "The LORD plagued Pharaoh and his house with great plagues because of Sarai" (Genesis 12:17). The word translated "plagued" here differs from the one used in Exodus where the ten plagues are described. The word here means basically "to touch"—and it can be used in a positive or negative sense.

I point this out because there's a bit of irony here. On the one hand, we have Abraham, the great man of God, who has left family, friends, and business behind to seek contact with God. On the other we have Pharaoh, who considers himself divine and feels very little need of contact with the God that Abraham seeks. And who really gets "in touch" with God? Pharaoh!

What's happening here? Why is God able to get through to the heathen king, when all His calls to Abraham seem to get a busy signal? Does God sometimes have to work through nonbelievers to reach His servants? Have you ever been brought up short on your spiritual journey by a so-called "heathen" who had a better sense of God's will than you? I know I have.

It's not hard to analyze what's going on here—because I've seen similar things happen in my own life and in the lives of other Christians. When you set out to follow the Lord, one of the traps the devil lays along the way for you is spiritual pride. "I'm God's man (or woman). God called me to this special ministry. That shows how much He trusts me. I've led us down this path, so it must be the right path. God wouldn't let me—His special, called servant—go astray. Follow me! I know the right way." As long as we're down in that pit of self-acclamation, we're out of range of God's guidance. It's not because God can't reach us there; the line's just busy with our own proud chatter, and we can't pay attention to two voices at once. Sometimes He has to knock a telephone pole down on our house to get us to shut up and listen!

HE DID IT AGAIN!

I can't imagine it seemed like good news when messengers from Pharaoh's palace came to Abraham's camp, summoning the patriarch and letting him in on the little secret that the king was holding him responsible for everything bad that had happened in his house for the past two months. It probably felt something like being hit by a falling telephone pole. Abraham must have followed them with fear and trembling.

But the amazing thing is that Pharaoh sensed the power of the God he was up against and decided he didn't want to incur any further misfortunes. (In this he showed a bit better judgment than his successor who held the throne when Moses and Aaron stopped by for a visit.) So he gave Sarah back and sent Abraham away without even asking him to return all the goodies he'd given him. "Then Abram went up from Egypt, he and his wife and all that he had, and Lot with him, to the South. Abram was very rich in livestock, in silver, and in gold" (Genesis 13:1, 2).

What did Abraham learn from this experience?

It depends on just how you read his story. Personally, I happen to think that there's one part of the story as it's told in Genesis that's misplaced in the sequence of events in Abraham's life. It's the story told in Genesis 20 of Abraham, Sarah, and King Abimelech of Gerar. It's virtually a duplicate of what happened in Egypt. Abraham gets scared again, gives his wife to a foreign king, and God has to miraculously deliver her back to her rightful husband.

There are serious problems with leaving that story where it is in the narrative of Abraham's life. This adventure with Abimelech has to be fit into a very tight space between the time the Lord promises the birth of Isaac and the time the following year when Isaac was born. That is, either one year after the visit or in the spring of the coming year. The upshot is that the events in Gerar all have to be wedged into a maximum twelve-month time span, probably less.

JOURNEY TO MORIAH

Maybe that's a doable, but there's another problem. In order for us to be sure Isaac is Abraham's son, not Abimelech's, the whole encounter with Sarah being taken into Abimelech's harem has to take place in one or two months after the Lord's promise to Abraham. Any longer, and Sarah would have been living with Abimelech nine months before Isaac was born—and just imagine the scandal that would cause! Abimelech could say whatever he wanted about not touching Sarah, but the tongues would still wag!

But there's even more information in the story that makes it impossible to fit into the short time allowed. At the conclusion, when Abimelech restores Sarah to Abraham, the patriarch prays that Abimelech's household be healed of the affliction that's come upon them "for the LORD had closed up all the wombs of the house of Abimelech because of Sarah, Abraham's wife" (Genesis 20:18).

How long does it take to figure out that all the wombs in your family have been closed? In other words, how long does it take to figure out that none of the women can get pregnant? Today, with the little blue test strips, you can find out whether or not you're pregnant within a few weeks. It took a bit longer back then—at least two or three months to be certain. So we're not talking about any fortnight sojourn of Sarah in Abimelech's harem. She had to be there long enough for them to notice that absolutely nobody in the whole tribe was having any luck making babies. That would probably take several months.

So it seems to me Abraham's second abandonment of his wife needs to be fit somewhere else in the story. And we haven't even addressed the question of why in the world Abimelech would be stealing a ninety-year-old postmenopausal woman in the first place. I mean, I can accept the idea that maybe Sarah looked really great late in life. But I wonder how much of a catch even Sophia Loren or Goldie Hawn will be at age ninety!

Having considered the difficulties of fitting the story where it's placed in Genesis, it's time to consult a map. Where is Gerar? Well, it just happens to be right along the very road a man on his way from Egypt to Bethel would take. And Genesis 13 says Bethel was Abraham's next destination. In Abraham's day it was an important caravan center, the first stop after the desert for travelers northbound from Egypt. Thus it would have been natural for Abraham to stop there on his way back to Canaan.

Geographically, Gerar fits very well into chapter 13, but it doesn't fit well anywhere else in the story. So I happen to think that the only thing Abraham learned in Egypt was that selling your wife is a great way to get rich! Apparently he tried it again in Gerar on his way north.

Did you ever get caught with your hand in the cookie jar two days in a row when you were a kid? What did your mom do the first time? Bake you a whole batch of cookies? I doubt it. But even if she did, what did she do the next day when she found you filching again? Bake you an even bigger batch? Not likely.

Even God doesn't usually behave that way. He's gracious all right— full of grace. But it's a rare thing to find Him rewarding people for bad behavior. Yet that's what He did for Abraham.

Imagine God delivering him twice in a row from the same stupid, self-serving gambit—and blessing him with rich gifts both times! But that's what He did. When Abimelech returned Sarah, he sent along sheep, oxen, male and female servants, plus a thousand pieces of silver!

It's hard to understand. I mean, how did God expect Abraham to learn the right things from his experience if he kept getting rewarded for bad behavior? But, as we'll see as we read on in the story, God's methodology worked.

The Lord had big plans for Abraham *and* Sarah. But the male half of this dynamic duo just didn't get it at first. So in a sense, God's kindness to Abraham was a bit of a slap in the face—a rebuke for trying to do things his own way instead of relying on God. Abraham was looking to Sarah to be his savior, and all the while the real Savior was watching, waiting, hoping to see faith take root, sprout up, and grow strong in Abraham's heart. And do you know what? It finally did.

There are a lot of lessons we can take away from this part of the story. One I hadn't thought of before this trip through the account is that God often allows blessings to come to His wayward children in hopes that the blessings will woo His children back to Him. We sometimes complain to the Lord, "Why do the wicked prosper?" (see Jeremiah 12:1 for example). But the Lord has His own inscrutable ways.

It took a couple undeserved windfall blessings for Abraham to learn what he needed to. But guess what: God knew what He was doing all along.

CHAPTER NINE

Blessings

"He went on his journey from the South as far as
Bethel, to the place where his tent had been at the
beginning, between Bethel and Ai, to the place of
the altar which he had made there at first. And
there Abram called on the name of the LORD.
"Lot also, who went with Abram, had flocks and
herds and tents. Now the land was not able to support them, that they might dwell together, for their
possessions were so great that they could not dwell
together. And there was strife between the herdsmen
of Abram's livestock and the herdsmen of Lot's
livestock. The Canaanites and the Perizzites then
dwelt in the land.
"So Abram said to Lot, 'Please let there be no strife
between you and me, and between my herdsmen and
your herdsmen; for we are brethren. Is not the whole
land before you? Please separate from me. If you take
the left, then I will go to the right; or, if you go to the
right, then I will go to the left' " (Genesis 13:3-9).

We're back to square three now. Square one was Haran; square two
was Shechem, where Abraham met God face to face. Square three is
Bethel—the place where Abraham built an altar and called out to God
but got no answer.

Blessings

By the time he and Lot and company had gotten that far, they were having serious problems. God had been entirely too good to them.

They may have been planning to go on as far north as Shechem—to get back to square two. But by the time they reached Bethel, it became obvious that traveling together just wasn't going to work. The reason given for the big split-up is that Lot's and Abraham's servants couldn't get along with each other. You can picture them staking out pasturage at every stop and bickering over who'd get the best spot each time, can't you?

I wonder if something else wasn't involved too. I get the feeling something pretty bad must have happened up in Shechem on the way through—because even after Lot leaves, Abraham never goes back there to live. Maybe there was a major confrontation with the inhabitants that didn't turn out well, who knows? If that's the case, it could help explain why the tension ran so high when the travelers got as far as Bethel. Maybe Abraham had resolved to go back to Shechem—the place he'd met and talked with God. But the closer they got, the antsier the servants became. They just didn't want to go back there. And because everyone's nerves were on edge, the usual bickering escalated to the point where something had to be done.

So Abraham and Lot take a little stroll along the backbone ridge, up to a place where they can see in all directions, and Abraham offers his young nephew first pick of everything. Rather out of character for Abraham, wouldn't you say? I mean, up to this point anyone getting into an argument with him could have pointed a finger at him and used that classic line, "It's all about *you*, isn't it, Abraham?"

Think about it. Nobody else has had any part to play in any of his earlier decisions. Abraham claims to hear God calling him to leave Haran, and nobody can dissuade him. What he's decided to do he does, taking along all his dependents plus Lot. They get to Shechem, and he decides to leave. They get to Egypt and Gerar, and Sarah's wishes don't seem to count for anything with him. But now all of a sudden, Lot gets first pick. Something's obviously changed about Abraham.

That's the neat thing about a spiritual journey. It forces you to grow. All of a sudden, Abraham's willing to depend on God rather than on himself.

It's not that he quit doing things his own way from then on or that he gave up working to make his business prosper. But he had learned something from his mistakes: that his scheming, no matter how smart or tricky, brought him no blessings that could even begin to compare with what the grace of God handed to him. And what must have really amazed him was how God insisted on blessing him even when he blew it and failed to trust. God had continued to bless him in spite of his best efforts to go it alone and provide his own blessings. Abraham had tried to run his own life, and even though he went on a five-hundred-mile detour into Egypt, God didn't let him far out of His sight. So Abraham's offering the best land to Lot was just what God wanted to see.

SIGNIFICANT CHOICES

As Abraham and Lot looked over the land from up there in the rocky hills by Bethel, Lot saw a place that looked like home. The Jordan valley reminded him of Haran and Ur—a place by a river where he could grow crops and find good pasture. And that memory of the fertile land where they had crossed the Jordan on the way to Shechem popped out of the place in the back of his mind where he had stored it away. Life would be a little less challenging in a fertile valley like that, he thought. So off he went, down into the valley, finally ending up near Sodom—not realizing how many spiritual challenges he would meet there.

Abraham, on the other hand, stayed at Bethel, at the altar where he had shouted at the silent skies and received no reply. But this time God was ready to meet with him there.

What made the difference? Had God changed? Or was it Abraham who had changed?

By leaving Shechem and setting out willfully to solve his own problems, Abraham had tuned God out. And even though he stopped in Bethel long enough to build an altar and call out to God, the Lord could see that he was just going through the motions.

Blessings

The fact that you go to church every week and bring your offerings and sing your praises and say your prayers doesn't necessarily mean you're really walking with God. In fact, religion sometimes gets in the way of true openness with God. It can make you feel secure—like everything's OK between you and God just because you went through the right rituals. But underneath the religious veneer you might be just as sneaky and conniving as the man who went to Egypt and sold his wife for profit.

So the problem at Bethel the first time Abraham passed through hadn't necessarily meant God had left him. God hadn't retreated to His throne in heaven and said, "You think I'm going to move down to Bethel with you? No way! I said Shechem's the place, and that's where I'm staying!" No, the problem was with Abraham.

So, when Abraham got back to Bethel, God came to meet him there—because Abraham, not God, had changed! Abraham was more willing to listen now. He'd had a chance to try things his own way, to chart his own path, to conjure self-created schemes, and none of it had done him a bit of good. Nothing had worked out according to his plans. He was still stuck with his barren wife, and he was back in Canaan—the land God had promised to him. And so God came to talk to him.

"Lift up your eyes," He said. (Lot had looked *down* into the valley; God tells Abraham to look *up*. Lot ends up living near the lowest point on earth, more than nine hundred feet below sea level; Abraham stays above it all, up on the heights. There's a sermon here, but we won't let it sidetrack us just now.)

God continues:

> "Look from the place where you are—northward, southward, eastward, and westward; for all the land which you see I give to you and your descendants forever. And I will make your descendants as the dust of the earth; so that if a man could number the dust of the earth, then your descendants also could be numbered. Arise, walk in the land through its length and its width, for I give it to you" (Genesis 13:14-17).

Wow! Did you pick up on the difference between this promise and the one Abraham received at Shechem? Up there at Shechem it was, "To your descendants I will give this land." Now it's, "All the land you see I give to *you* and your descendants." And this from the God who has done so much to bless him already. Things are definitely starting to look up for Abraham. Everything he can see is now his for the claiming. Talk about blessings!

But notice what Abraham does about it: "Then Abram moved his tent, and went and dwelt by the terebinth trees of Mamre, which are in Hebron, and built an altar there to the Lord" (Genesis 13:18).

Hebron's a good two-day's journey—maybe three days for a large group—south of Bethel. And what runs through my mind is, *Why south, Abraham? Why do you insist on going south from Bethel instead of up north to Shechem?* But I don't know the whole story, so I can't judge. It was in Shechem that Abraham noticed that the Canaanites were already on the land God was promising to him; if he didn't feel that was the way to go, who am I to judge?

God had encouraged him to take a walking tour of all the land, north, south, east, and west—kind of to lay claim to it in the name of his God. But apparently Abraham was satisfied to head south. Maybe he was just plain tired of walking and figured he'd leave the gift in God's capable hands until he needed it. Or maybe he'd seen something at Hebron that he liked. There were some big trees there—trees like the one where he'd met God at Shechem. So that's where he took up residence.

CHAPTER TEN

Babylon

"It came to pass in the days of Amraphel king of Shinar, Arioch king of Ellasar, Chedorlaomer king of Elam, and Tidal king of nations, that they made war with Bera king of Sodom, Birsha king of Gomorrah, Shinab king of Admah, Shemeber king of Zeboiim, and the king of Bela (that is, Zoar). . . .

"Then they took all the goods of Sodom and Gomorrah, and all their provisions, and went their way. They also took Lot, Abram's brother's son who dwelt in Sodom, and his goods, and departed.

"Then one who had escaped came and told Abram the Hebrew, for he dwelt by the terebinth trees of Mamre the Amorite, brother of Eshcol and brother of Aner; and they were allies with Abram. Now when Abram heard that his brother was taken captive, he armed his three hundred and eighteen trained servants who were born in his own house, and went in pursuit as far as Dan. He divided his forces against them by night, and he and his servants attacked them and pursued them as far as Hobah, which is north of Damascus. So he brought back all the goods, and also brought back his brother Lot and his goods, as well as the women and the people" (Genesis 14:1, 2, 11-16).

JOURNEY TO MORIAH

Just as soon as God gives you something, the enemy's sure to show up and try to take it away from you. If you thought that setting out to follow God was going to be a stroll in the park, think again. Whenever you get into a close relationship with God and start receiving blessings from Him, you'll start facing challenges too.

There are several lessons here. Let's start by looking at Lot. What's he doing in the story anyway? Why did he come along with Abraham on this quest to know God? Was it for spiritual reasons? For adventure? Because he liked his uncle? Because he'd had a fight with the rest of the family back home? Was he a spiritual seeker himself or just along for the ride? We're never told Lot's reasoning.

Are you a genuine spiritual seeker or just a tagalong who hopes to somehow benefit from others' spiritual quests? Do you like to get into the Bible and study it for yourself? When you go to church, do you like to be part of a Bible study class where members feel free to share and learn together from each others' experiences, study, and struggles? Do you find yourself constantly asking God, "What's next? What more would You have me do? What new thing do You want to teach me?" Or do you prefer to just go to church once a week, hear a sermon, and hope to pick up some spiritual crumbs from someone else's quest?

We never hear anything about Lot building an altar or talking with God. He seems like a mere camp follower with no significant part in the story until he either causes problems or gets into trouble—which is about to happen, because "Abram dwelt in the land of Canaan, and Lot dwelt in the cities of the plain and pitched his tent even as far as Sodom. But the men of Sodom were exceedingly wicked and sinful against the Lord" (Genesis 13:12, 13). Whenever you read about wicked and sinful people in the Bible, you can be sure that trouble's not far away. Either they're going to cause trouble or they're about to get into trouble.

The geography involved in Lot's selection of land and the ensuing invasion is fascinating, both spiritually and physically. What in the world do I mean by spiritual geography, you ask? Just this: The kings who attacked Sodom came from the area Abraham was told to leave—up to the north. Shinar in particular always gets bad press in the Bible because it stands for opposition to God. Compare this story with the events described in Genesis 10:10 and Daniel 1:2, for example. Shinar is the place where those in rebellion against God built the Tower of Babel. And when God's people failed to repent of their sins in the days of Daniel, the king of Babylon attacked and carried away goods and people "into the land of Shinar to the house of his god" (Daniel 1:2).

The book of Ezra tells the story of a time thirteen centuries down the road when God's faithful remnant who had been carried away captive to the land of Shinar/Babylon were called to leave and go to the land their ancestor Abraham had been given. Those who were willing to walk by faith answered the call to come out of Babylon. And near the end of Bible times, the apostle John hears an angel from heaven crying out, "Babylon the great is fallen, is fallen. . . . Come out of her, my people, lest you share in her sins, and lest you receive of her plagues" (Revelation 18:2, 4.) This call is to God's people at the end of time to come out of apostate religions and learn to rely in total faith on Him instead of on themselves.

BACKTRACKING

What we learn from Genesis 14 is that the Jordan valley, where Lot took up residence, had been under the control of kings from the area of Babylon for the past dozen years. In other words, when Lot looked out over the valley and it reminded him of home—the well-watered valleys of Ur and Haran—he chose to backtrack on his journey. He cast aside any spiritual progress he had made while following Abraham in favor of the well-watered valley. In essence he went back to Babylon the day he parted company with his uncle. When Amraphel, Arioch, Chedorlaomer, and Tidal came and took him captive and started marching him back toward Babylon proper, it was only the confirmation of a decision he had already made. So the lesson we can learn from the spiritual geography here is that when you quit moving ahead with the Lord, you start going backward— immediately. Your regression may not be obvious at first. But if you've stepped onto self-serving, rebellious ground, the king of Babylon will be along one day to make sure you know you're his captive.

The physical geography of the story is interesting too. Reading the list of cities the kings ravaged on their way to Sodom reveals that they marched their armies down the same King's Highway that Abraham had followed from Haran. But they didn't cross over to the west side of the Jordan. That was a smart move on their part, because Egypt considered the territory on that side of the river to be under her control. If the kings had come over to the side where Abraham was living, they would have risked a confrontation with Pharaoh. Because it seems likely that a fairly small band of soldiers carried out this raid, an encounter with Pharaoh's armies probably wasn't on their preferred agenda.

When Abraham went to rescue Lot, Genesis 14:14 says Abraham "armed his three hundred and eighteen trained servants." The word translated "servants" is *hanikim*, a word that occurs only once in the Bible, but apparently is of Egyptian origin. So it's just possible that much of his army was made up of Egyptian soldiers he got from Pharaoh (Genesis 12:16), and that when he attacked the kings as they headed home with their booty, one of the reasons they turned out to be such pushovers was that they thought the Egyptian army had fallen upon them. Because the Egyptians were in the habit of keeping small garrisons of troops in areas they sought to control, local rulers Aner and Eshcol, who went with Abraham, may have had some Egyptians in their service as well.

(I know that Genesis 14:14 says Abraham's servants "were born in his own house," but chapter 15:3 says the same of Eliezer, who obviously was born in Damascus. The concept conveyed by this expression seems to be that the men in question are children—or servants—of Abraham's own house, not necessarily that they were physically born there. In Mesopotamia, servants were often regarded as part of the extended family of the head of a clan.)

The point of all this is that the physical geography of the foreign kings' raid fits well with what we know of the geopolitical situation in Abraham's day. Elam, home of Chedorlaomer, was in a period of ascendancy at the time, having played a key role in the overthrow of the Third Dynasty of Ur a few years earlier. The name *Tidal* is recognized by scholars as a Hebrew rendition of the Hittite name Tudhalias. But Anatolia was not yet under the control of a central Hittite king. The records of the Assyrian merchants who lived in the area at that time refer to chiefs and paramount chiefs as the rulers. If Tidal was one of these paramount chiefs with a number of other chiefs under him, the description "king of nations" would fit well. It's not clear exactly where "Arioch king of Ellasar" came from, but the name Arriwuk has been found on clay tablets discovered in the Mesopotamian city of Mari, which was the capital of a powerful kingdom at this time and controlled all trade going up and down the middle part of the Euphrates river.

With proper irrigation, the hot region around the river Jordan can produce rich crops. Today, farmers in the area produce three crops of tomatoes per year because there is no end to the growing season. There are also huge date groves and banana plantations in the valley. Excavations in the area of Bab edh-Dhra on the eastern shore of the Dead Sea give evidence of a flourishing civilization centered on five "cities of the plain," at least two of which were destroyed by a fiery conflagration. Archaeologists think they were inhabited only during the three centuries before Abraham's sojourn, and that no one was living there while he was in Hebron, so these may not be the same cities of the plain mentioned in the story of Lot. Nonetheless the cities do at least give us an idea of what life must have been like for Abraham's nephew down in the valley.

In addition to agricultural wealth, the towns probably served as trading centers dealing in tar from the Dead Sea and copper from mines in the Sinai. The pharaohs of Egypt's Twelfth Dynasty had recently reopened those mines in Abraham's day, so trade was probably flowing strongly through Sodom and on up the King's Highway.

Such a rich area naturally attracted the attention of the coalition of kings who controlled the Euphrates valley to the north and east of Canaan. They sent raiding parties through the area periodically to seize the produce of the inhabitants' labors and to place the conquered people under tribute. But, as usually happens eventually with people in a "taxation without representation" situation, rebellion soon began to brew. It came to a head not long after Lot arrived.

THE SITTING DUCK

Lot doesn't seem to have gotten involved in the pitched battle fought in the Valley of Siddim. But when the local kings lost and fled to the mountains, he was left a sitting duck and ended up being taken captive. That means he was doomed to be a slave in Babylon for the rest of his life. I guess the moral here is that you don't have to cast your lot fully with the wicked to end up suffering with them. Just hanging out with them is enough to buy you a trainload of trouble.

Satisfied with the success of their raid, the kings from the north took their spoils and headed back toward Babylon. But they had not reckoned with the power of God as it is manifested in one who has answered His call. When Abraham heard about Lot's predicament, he knew he had to do something about it. He couldn't just sit back and say, "Too bad what happened to Lot. Serves him right for choosing what looked like the best land!"

Neither did Abraham consider it sufficient to call his clan together and have special prayer for Lot and his neighbors: "Dear Lord, we have received tidings that thou hast allowed thy servant and our dear friend Lot to go into captivity to serve the vile and evil Babylonians. We do pray that thou wouldst be with him in this hour of his trial, and thou wouldst uphold and sustain him, that he may be a witness for thee even in these dire and evil circumstances that thou hast allowed to come upon him. For we know that thou dost love him and that thou wilt bless him even in this extremity."

Abraham was still learning just how to walk well with God. He would still stumble from time to time, taking things into his own hands when he shouldn't have. But he saw this situation as one that clearly required action. Quick action. Without hesitating, he went on the offensive to save his wayward nephew. He called a council of war, gathered his Amorite allies, provisioned his own troop, and marched northward in pursuit of the raiders.

The victorious kings from the north had planned their campaign well. On their way south, they had destroyed all effective resistance along their path all the way from Damascus, then had swept around and wiped out anyone who might attack them from the rear. The list of places they defeated is given in Genesis 14:5-7. Only after they had cleared a wide path for their return journey did they attack the cities of the plain that had formed an alliance against them.

Babylon

Then, loaded down with booty, they began their trip home—no doubt traveling a bit slower than they had on their blitzkrieg trip south. There were newly captured slaves to march along on foot, and they'd probably stashed additional spoils in the areas they'd conquered previously, so they had to stop and pick up those things, burdening themselves down even more. That gave Abraham and his allies a bit of time to get organized, march north, and get in position to raid the raiders. The scouts found them near Dan, north of the Sea of Galilee. Abraham and company probably watched the victorious raiders party hearty well into the night, then attacked from two sides when most of the soldiers were snoring off a drunken stupor. "He divided his forces against them by night, and he and his servants attacked them and pursued them as far as Hobah, which is north of Damascus" (Genesis 14:15).

Abraham's force wasn't large enough to completely surround and overpower the army he attacked, but the midnight reveille apparently panicked them enough to start them running. Then Abraham's small, mobile force continued to pursue and attack the heavily laden caravan on its way northward for more than forty miles, even past Damascus. The kings from the north were forced to flee for their lives, dropping loot all along the way.

On their trip home, Abraham and his allies, Aner, Eshcol, and Mamre, met Melchizedek, king of Salem. Melchizedek's name means "my king is righteousness." Not only was he a king, but he was also "priest of God Most High" (*El Elyon*).

Melchizedek is an enigma. He dwelt there among the Canaanites, yet was a king of righteousness and peace who knew the God who created heaven and earth. Christian interpreters see in him a foreshadowing of Christ, and some even go so far as to say that he was some sort of a preincarnation of Jesus. That seems a bit of a stretch to me. He certainly did play a fascinating role in this story, though, and the bread and wine perhaps in some way prefigure the Last Supper.

Melchizedek isn't mentioned anywhere else in the story. He simply comes on the scene here and then disappears from history.

His sudden appearance at the Valley of Shaveh (probably the Kidron Valley on the east side of Jerusalem) didn't surprise Abraham though.

Somehow the patriarch was already acquainted with this king of peace and righteousness. And somehow he had come to accept Melchizedek as a person he could look to for spiritual blessings.

Salem is apparently the Jebusite city that King David later renamed Jerusalem. Because it is on the main road between Bethel and Hebron, Abraham must have passed through it at least three times before his military march to catch the kings from the north. So, when he headed out on this dangerous mission, do you suppose he stopped in Salem and sought Melchizedek's blessing on his endeavor—maybe even asked for the priest's counsel? That could explain Melchizedek's sudden appearance when Abraham is returning home. Perhaps Abraham saw him as a kindred spirit because they were both seekers after the "Most High God."

It's often difficult for spiritual pilgrims—especially men—to find suitable traveling companions. For a man like Abraham, who had exercised extreme courage in stepping out to follow wherever God would lead, it was probably especially hard to find a spiritual peer, let alone someone he would trust as a guide or mentor. Lot had not proved to be that kind of companion. Somehow, though, Melchizedek must have fulfilled that role.

Abraham recognizes in Melchizedek a person worthy of his respect, and Melchizedek recognizes in Abraham a man especially blessed of God, and he wants to affirm God's blessing with a ceremony. So he comes out to meet the returning warriors, bringing bread and wine with him. Then he pronounces a blessing upon Abraham. "Blessed be Abram of God Most High," he says, and then he further identifies this God whom Abraham and he worship as "Possessor of heaven and earth" (Genesis 14:19). Many translations render this "Creator of heaven and earth" because the Hebrew word used implies both construction and acquisition of something. It's the verb Eve used when she had her first baby: "I've acquired a man from the LORD," she said. But for the past nine months or so, she'd had quite a lot to do with the acquiring!

After blessing Abraham, Melchizedek praises God: "Blessed be God Most High, Who has delivered your enemies into your hand" (verse 20). Sending praises and blessings both ways was the role of a priest or mediator, and Abraham apparently recognized this function of the enigmatic king as well. It was only natural, then, that he should offer a tithe of the spoils to the priest.

I think if I'd been in Abraham's shoes, I would have taken it for granted that this whole adventure had been part of God's plan to make me richer. I probably wouldn't have had any trouble giving Melchizedek his ten percent, but the rest—well, I wouldn't want to see the Sodomites left totally destitute and homeless, so I probably would have sent them home with enough basic provisions to get by. But having taken a big risk and spent a lot on travel expenses, I think I would have considered most of what I got on my raid as just a good return on investment.

But by now Abraham had learned something about God's way of blessing, and he wasn't about to keep anything that didn't belong to him. Verses 22 and 23 imply that even before the battle he'd promised God that he wouldn't keep any of the spoil. He let Aner, Eshcol, and Mamre enrich themselves, but he wanted to be sure that the glory for all he accomplished went to God. So he gave his portion back to its original owners and explained why—giving a clear and unequivocal testimony to the goodness of his God. What a marvelous opportunity this was for the Sodomites to inquire about God and perhaps begin to worship Him. But they missed their chance. They'd seen the grace of God at work in a powerful way. They would see it demonstrated one more time. Rejecting it the next time would seal their doom. And grace rejected would turn to wrath.

The next time we meet Abraham, he is back home, and he is shaking in his sandals. To make a lightning raid and bring the spoils home requires a lot of adrenalin—especially for an octogenarian. After his great spiritual high, after the victory at Dan and the inspiring worship service at Salem, Abraham found himself back home having second thoughts—probably wondering what he'd gotten himself into. He'd always gone to great lengths to live peacefully with people before—fleeing Shechem to avoid confrontation, giving up his wife instead of fighting for her. Now, suddenly, he's placed himself on the precarious ground of a warrior with at least four kings for enemies.

Scary.

CHAPTER ELEVEN

Remonstrance

"The word of the LORD came to Abram in a vision, saying, 'Do not be afraid, Abram. I am your shield, your exceedingly great reward.'
"But Abram said, 'Lord GOD, what will You give me, seeing I go childless, and the heir of my house is Eliezer of Damascus?' Then Abram said, 'Look, You have given me no offspring; indeed one born in my house is my heir!' " (Genesis 15:1-3).

Warfare in Abraham's day wasn't a matter of salaried soldiers going off to foreign lands to "make the world safe for democracy" or anything altruistic like that. War was waged for pillage and profit. Kings rode off to war because that was the quickest way to acquire the gold, silver, slaves, and other treasures kings liked to have to make themselves look good and powerful in the eyes of their people.

But Abraham's war had been altruistic from start to finish. He'd ridden out to rescue his nephew, and on his return he hadn't kept any of the spoils. Could it be that when all the adrenaline wore off, he started having second thoughts? As he watched Aner and Eshcol riding around on richly adorned donkeys and wearing fine Babylonian linens, did his own woolen robes begin to itch a little more than usual?

It's easy to fall into that kind of trap when you see your neighbor driving his new Jaguar. After all, he never goes to church, and he considers a $100 annual donation to the United Way a sign of his great generosity. Why should he be so blessed when all you can afford after you give your tithes and offerings is a second-hand Buick?

But God comes to Abraham with a message designed to nip that kind of thinking in the bud. "I'm your shield, Abraham, and I'm also your reward. The spoils of battle may look enticing, but they'll soon wear out. When Aner's new robe has gone to tatters, you'll still have Me."

And how does Abraham respond to God's munificent proclamation?

His response is almost scandalous on first glance. But let's take a closer look. It actually reveals that Abraham has grown by another leap and bound or two in his relationship with God.

Abraham essentially responds to God by throwing His promises back in His face. "Platitudes and promises—that's all I get from you!" he shouts. "When are you going to really give me something? When are you going to give me what I want? When are you going to give me a son?"

How do you feel about talking to God that way? Is it wise to question God? Is it safe to get angry with Him?

I walked out the emergency entrance of the hospital with Sister Elaine, the chaplain. We had just ministered to a family whose eight-year-old son had died. His teenage sister had rolled the family car on icy roads, and the boy had been thrown out and suffered a broken neck.

"I have a feeling I'm going to go home and be very angry at God tonight," Elaine said. Her remark caught me off guard. I didn't know how to respond. I couldn't remember ever being angry at God. There had been times when I had abandoned God, even denied His existence. I had ignored Him and disobeyed Him, but I couldn't remember being angry at Him. After all, what good would it do? He is God and I am His creation; I must simply accept His sovereign will. At least that's the way I was raised. What God does is not something you argue about with Him any more than you argue with your dad and mom about their getting married and having children.

I've come to realize that I was wrong about that. I've come to realize that for Abraham, the ability to argue with God was a step in the right direction.

JOURNEY TO MORIAH

Abraham had been through the stage of ignoring God, had progressed from there to listening, and from there to trusting. But when he learned to argue with God, it meant he had taken a step toward acknowledging God's sovereignty on a whole new level.

You never argue with a traffic light. It wouldn't change no matter what you said. But if a living, breathing policeman is directing traffic at an intersection—well, a little arguing or pleading might change his mind if your wife's in the back seat about ready to pop with a new addition to your family. Before Abraham could argue with God, he had to learn to quit treating Him like a stop-and-go light. He had to learn to respond to the mind of God, not just the will of God. Do you see the difference?

A BOOK OF ANSWERS

I've known people who think of the Bible as a book of answers—about like a pack of Tarot cards. When they want answers, they go looking for a one-verse text that will give them a simple yes or no that precludes the need for reasoning and short-circuits the need for prayer. There's no need for wrestling with God, for trying to determine what greater growth He would like them to experience. All they want is an answer.

Of course, if you can't find just the right answer by *reading* the Bible, you can always resort to the old point-and-pick routine: Let the Bible fall open to a random page, close your eyes, and point. Whatever verse comes up—there's your answer. This method turns God's Word into some sort of magical oracle, giving directives that don't require any rational thought or interaction with the advice giver. You might as well throw dice or pick an answer by the eeny-meeny-miney-mo method.

Up to this point Abraham had always looked to God for stop-and-go answers—as though all God wanted from their relationship was a submissive, unquestioning slave. But God obviously wanted something much more, because when Abraham responded with remonstrance instead of resignation, God stuck around, continued the conversation, and moved the relationship with His friend to a whole new level. And suddenly Abraham began to discover the difference between blind obedience and walking in faith with a rational, reasonable God.

In Abraham's previous communications with God, God did the talking and Abraham did the listening. No real communication was established—only one-way instruction. In Genesis 15, however, we read that when God came to Abraham to promise him protection and a very great reward, Abraham answered back. He had finally gotten over his amazement and awe at the thought that God would indeed speak to him. He'd had time to think over God's promises. He'd had time to try to help God out by getting rid of his barren wife. But what he'd done so far hadn't worked out very well. For one thing, it hadn't produced any children. And every time he'd tried to solve the problem himself, God had gently overruled and blessed him in the process—demonstrating that He, God, really didn't need much help from Abraham. It was a pretty one-sided relationship, dominated by God.

Abraham had experienced his own helplessness in the hand of God, as well as the great power that God could give him. He had marched out to rescue Lot after covenanting not to keep the spoils—thereby assuring that he was doing it for God's glory, not his own. Marching by faith, he had discovered God's faithfulness not only in preserving his life but also in giving him victory. Now he wanted God to begin to work with him in a new way. He had found the Most High to be a close enough Friend that he was willing to bank on that friendship and trust that it would endure a little argument. So when God announced that Abraham's reward would be very great, the patriarch had a few questions he wanted to ask.

Abraham couldn't see that God was really doing anything but talking. "Do you really think I'll be satisfied to see you bless the children of my adopted son, Eliezer?" he asked. "It's *my* kids I want you to bless, and you haven't even bothered to give me any yet. Promises, promises is all I get."

Have you ever been that frustrated with God? Have you ever looked up at the sky and shouted, "Where are you, Jesus? You said You were coming *quickly!* Is two thousand years *quickly* in Your book?" Have you ever looked through tear-filled eyes at the casket of a loved one whose healing you fasted and prayed for, and then muttered under your breath,

"What was that all about, God? Didn't You promise that You'd heal people we prayed for and anointed?"

Or have you felt like you had no right to question God? That your proper role in relation to Him is silent submission?

If Abraham's interaction with God in Genesis 15 teaches me anything, it is that God doesn't mind being questioned. In fact, He seems to relish it. He's not an autocratic dictator whose thoughts cannot be questioned. He's a loving, personal God who wants to interact on a rational level with His creation. Why else would He have given us minds and the power to reason?

When Abraham called God on His promises, God moved their relationship to a new level. Now He could go beyond sending "go" and "stop" messages to His friend. He could begin to be more specific in His promises. "Eliezer will not be your heir," He said. "You will have a son of your own as heir, and your descendants will be as numerous as the stars in the sky."

ABRAHAM'S FAITH GROWS

Now that Abraham had discovered that he could really communicate with God, his faith grew by a great leap. Despite the fact that Sarah was growing old, Abraham believed God's promise of a multitude of heirs. That's what God wanted. That's what God counted as rightness with Him. Simple trust.

Leaving home, family, almost everything behind and wandering under God's leadership for a thousand miles or so didn't make Abraham righteous.

Going to battle and rescuing Lot from Babylonian captivity—doing evangelism in its most challenging setting ever—didn't make Abraham righteous.

Giving back the spoils of war to those who had been raided didn't make Abraham righteous.

Tithing didn't make Abraham righteous.

Trusting is what made Abraham righteous. Trusting in the face of his own overwhelming doubts—doubts so profound that he didn't mind expressing them in the very presence of God. Abraham was a thinking, questioning seeker now. And these new ingredients strengthened his relationship with God.

From what I've learned, I don't think I can emphasize this point too strongly. There are many ways to know God—many levels on which we can come to know Him. But I honestly don't think a relationship can grow as deep and strong as God would like it to be without visiting the thinking, questioning, arguing stage. The very fact that I was so surprised by Sister Elaine's anger at God was an indication that I hadn't trodden very far along Abraham's path yet. I was still afraid to question God, and that meant my relationship with Him was still based more on fear than on love, because as John, the be*loved* disciple, put it, "Love has been perfected among us in this: that we may have boldness in the day of judgment; because as He is, so are we in this world. There is no fear in love; but perfect love casts out fear. . . . But he who fears has not been made perfect in love" (1 John 4:17, 18).

The day of judgment is the day we face God. And when Abraham faced God in vision, he had the boldness to ask questions and call God up short on what he considered unfulfilled promises.

And guess what. That's what God had been looking for all along in Abraham. A two-way relationship of trust. Now God had someone He could really communicate with, someone to imbibe of His goodness and become like Him. And because the way was now open for Abraham to be filled with God's goodness, God considered the filling an accomplished fact—the trust became the righteousness because it opened the way for the filling with righteousness. Now the man who had spent so many years doing things his own way was open to really listen, to challenge what he heard, and to learn. He had moved from rote learning to really getting to know his subject—God. And because God could see the progress, He was willing to give Abraham an "A" in the subject. He knew what the outcome of such learning would be.

Then God renewed the promise He had made just after Abraham let Lot take the best-looking pastureland. "I've called you here to give this land to you," He said.

Abraham, emboldened by the response he'd gotten so far, responded with another question: "He said, 'Lord GOD, how shall I know that I will inherit it?' " (verse 8).

God's answer seems odd, unless you understand the customs of the day. He simply instructed Abraham to bring him a cow, a goat, a ram, a turtledove, and a pigeon. Abraham understood what to do with them. He killed each of them, then divided all but the birds into two halves, and laid them out on the ground to see what would happen. He waited all afternoon and into the evening. When vultures began to circle and dive, he drove them away. He knew what he was waiting for, and he was determined that nothing would interfere.

As the sun touched the horizon, his eyes grew heavy. He could no longer stay awake. In his sleep he heard a voice speaking to him, promising that although things would be hard for his descendants for several generations, in the end God would indeed give this land to them. But that was just words again. It wasn't what Abraham was waiting for.

When he awoke, he discovered that the carcasses had not been disturbed while he slept. Something had protected them from the beasts. And then in the pitch darkness of a moonless night, under the stars that God had challenged him to number, Abraham saw and heard what he'd been waiting for. Untouched by human hands, a smoking firepot and a flaming torch appeared. Abraham watched in awe as these symbols of God Himself passed silently by and took their stand between the pieces of the carcasses. Then God spoke again, this time in the form of a solemn covenant oath.

This is the first we hear of God making a covenant with Abraham. Always before it had been a promise or a call. But now God was willing to bind Himself in solemn covenant to Abraham and his descendants. "I will give this land to your descendants," He covenanted.

Because of where God stood to make this covenant, Abraham knew now that he wasn't just hearing things and that God wasn't making a revocable commitment. He'd asked how he could know for sure, and God had done the very thing that Abraham himself would do when making a solemn covenant. He had passed between the carcass halves.

Passing between the halves was a well-known way of solemnizing a covenant. It said, with graphic visual aids, "I stake my very life on my faithfulness to the covenant we have made today." The individuals making the covenant agreement invoked upon themselves the fate of the sacrificed beasts should they fail to make good their word. So, God had sworn by His very existence that Abraham's descendants would inherit the land of promise!

But there's something else significant in this visual imagery. Something's left out of the normal covenant ceremony. God didn't invite Abraham to pass between the halves with Him. For a covenant between two people to be properly ratified, both had to stand between the carcass halves. By His action in passing between the halves alone, God decreed that this covenant didn't depend on both parties. It depended only on Himself. Just as God protected the covenant carcasses while Abraham slept, so He would carry out the terms of the covenant whether or not Abraham remained faithful.

But God knew now that Abraham would be faithful, because the channels of communication had come open at last. God's faithfulness could now fill His servant.

Subsequent events would prove that even after a mountaintop high, a death valley low, and a revival by God Himself, Abraham's faith and communication were not perfect. And that Abraham himself was far from perfect. But did that annul the righteousness God had reckoned to him?

No.

God had now bound Himself by a life-and-death oath in His relationship to Abraham. And He—the eternal God of the universe—would move heaven and hell to make sure that His promises would be fulfilled. He would even go so far as to suffer and die to assure that His friends—those who entered into a relationship with Him like Abraham's—could be filled with His righteousness.

Imagine that! An omnipotent God who is willing to bind His own hands (or have them bound to a cross!) in order to maintain open channels of communication, blessing, and righteousness to His people.

It's a thought worth contemplating for all eternity, don't you think?

CHAPTER TWELVE

Fulfillment

"He said to Abram: 'Know certainly that your descendants will be strangers in a land that is not theirs, and will serve them, and they will afflict them four hundred years. And also the nation whom they serve I will judge; afterward they shall come out with great possessions.'" (Genesis 15:13, 14).

It really wasn't that great a promise, if you look at it closely. Isn't the following about what God said? "All right already, Abraham. You've been begging for kids for so long, I'll give them to you. Then I'll let your grandkids and great grandkids and great-great grandkids suffer a lot as slaves—some of them for their whole lives—but your great-great-great grandkids will get to go free with lots of goodies!"

I don't mean to sound sarcastic, but really, I don't think I would have been very excited about a promise like this. I mean, if I pray for the solution to a problem, I usually want it yesterday if not sooner. Why promise me something wonderful that's going to happen four or five generations from now? What good does that do *me?*

But Abraham seemed quite content with God's promise. At least he didn't argue any further; he just accepted it. Which says to me that I probably have a bit more growing up to do in my walk with God— because I was raised in the instant-gratification generation.

The baby boomers of postwar America have got to be some of the most impatient people ever to walk the face of this planet. We're the ones who've made millionaires of people like Colonel Sanders and Dave Thomas, who found ways to give us our lunch in sixty seconds or less. We're the first to consider it our birthright to be cured of serious infectious diseases in three days max. The first to figure that if a headache can't be deadened in twenty minutes or less, there's something wrong with the medication.

We don't pray about things we want our great-great-great-grandchildren to accomplish. Who are they, anyhow? They probably won't even know our names. (Let's see—do I know any of my sixteen great-great-great-grandfathers' names, or even where they lived? I don't think so.) In fact, we want Jesus to come before we grow old and crotchety because we're afraid we're going to have a hard time being patient with the help in the nursing home we don't want to end up in. "I want my walker *now*, not next week sometime!" Is that my gravelly old voice I hear echoing up and down those sterile halls?

So I don't think I would have been very excited by what God promised to Abraham. But it didn't seem to bother him a bit. Mainly, he wanted to be sure that he was indeed going to have children. However God wanted to do it and whatever He wanted to do with them were no concerns of Abraham, as long as he could have kids.

In the society of his time, having no children was a great disgrace. And studying the burial customs of the people he lived among reveals that provisions for the next life were an important consideration one wanted to be sure was properly attended to while one was alive.

Don't misunderstand me. I'm not saying that Abraham necessarily bought into the whole King Tut thing, in which you wanted your descendants to fill your grave with a Fort Knox-worth of good things that you could use on the other side of death. But the society and generation I was born into thoroughly color my expectations about life. I'm sure that Abraham couldn't help noticing that people around him thought less of him for having no children. Maybe people even went so far as to ask him who he thought was going to take care of his spirit after he died. It was the sons who were supposed to provide food, drink, and other offerings to sustain their father's spirit in the netherworld. Fathers who weren't provided for properly could be expected to come back to this world and haunt their descendants—and wreak havoc on other people as well. So the community wanted to make sure that all those who died had someone to take proper care of their spirits.

Maybe some of Abraham's friends came to him and suggested that he ought to consider taking another wife because Sarah was obviously an unfruitful field. Did some of his female slaves perhaps bat their eyes at him, knowing how frustrated he must be? How, exactly, *did* Hagar come to be in the picture? She's called Sarah's Egyptian handmaid. Did she come along as a bonus when Pharaoh sent Sarah back home to Abraham? Or did she come into the household in Egypt by Abraham's selection?

I don't mean to be naughty here or to always assume the worst of Abraham, but his walk with the Lord was a growing experience. Genesis 13 is the first place where we see him beginning to respond to God in faith on anything more than a rudimentary level. And his detour to Egypt occurred before that.

So, maybe Hagar was a girl Abraham had selected as one of several possibilities for being The One—the one who would help him fulfill all the promises God had given to him. The fertile field that would sprout up with life when watered. That's just a thought—a possibility to tuck into the back of your mind as we consider the scene at the breakfast table the morning after God's nighttime covenant with Abraham.

SARAH'S SACRIFICE

Sarah's been out of her tent early and seen the mess Abraham left— bloody animal parts marking the boundaries of a mysterious path. Abraham comes to the cooking fire for breakfast, and she looks at him with her hands on her hips. "So, who'd you make a covenant with last night?" she asks. "The servants told me you were cutting up some of the best livestock, but they said no one was around with whom to make a covenant."

"The Lord made a covenant with me," Abraham responds.

"Oh."

With that single word Sarah turns back to her morning chores. But the word speaks volumes: "I don't even want to hear about it, Abraham. It's the same old song and dance you've been giving me for years. Don't tell me, let me guess: He said something about blessing your children. *Children!* Don't even talk to me about it!"

The servants set Abraham's breakfast before him; but Sarah isn't there. She's gone to her tent to weep. Abraham finds her there after breakfast.

"He spoke to me again of descendants," he begins. "Of this whole land belonging to my descendants. And this time it was more than just a promise. He *covenanted* with me! Do you know what that means? The Lord Himself made a covenant!"

His words meet only a glassy, tear-drained stare.

"Perhaps we should try again tonight," he offers, and she gives a slight nod in response.

The servants notice that Abraham goes about the day's work with even more spring in his step than usual. Late in the afternoon, Sarah calls Hagar to her, and the two women secret themselves away inside Sarah's tent. Many words can be heard passing between the two women, but no one overhears enough to know just what kind of plan they are hatching.

A full moon rises at sunset, and earlier than usual Abraham leaves the circle of men who recline around the embers of the dying cooking fire. Only one small lamp burns in Sarah's tent, but when he enters he immediately senses that more than one person is inside. He looks questioningly at Sarah.

"See, I have given you my handmaid—according to the laws of the land," she says hastily. "Perhaps she will give you the descendants God has promised." And with that she slips out of the tent and vanishes into the ominous, expectant silence of the night.

What is Abraham to do? What can he fall back upon but the promises of God for the future and his experiences of the past?

The promises tell him that he will have a son. The experiences remind him that Sarah has not been able to be the channel of God's blessings. Yet God has rebuked all his attempts to be rid of her.

It's her idea this time. It's not any infringement on her dignity. It's her choice, and perhaps this is what God has been waiting for—for the woman who stands in the way of the promise to step aside and let God work. And so he sleeps with Hagar. And falls back into the old trap of depending on human plans and human strengths to fulfill God's plans.

What member of my baby-boom generation or their children or grandchildren who have been raised to expect instant results could blame Abraham and Sarah for wanting to hurry things along? It had been ten long years since they'd left Haran with dreams of bouncing babies putting a new twinkle in their eyes. How much patience were they supposed to have?

Why do God's promises so often tarry? My generation struggles repeatedly with the issue we call "the delay of the advent." Our great-great-great-great grandparents had a bright twinkle in their eyes as they anticipated the return of Jesus in 1844. And when the event still had not occurred half a century later, they published books like *Prophecies of Jesus, Illustrated* to reassure their children and grandchildren that even though much time had passed and Jesus still hadn't returned, things certainly were shaping up now for a quick climax to earth's history. In a book published in 1897, J. G. Matteson quoted a Lutheran paper to buttress his hope of a soon Advent: " 'How fast events are developing in this century! Does it not look as though the great drama of the world is nearing its close so that every minute we may expect to see the curtain drop?' "[1]

Matteson went on to cite events such as the June 17, 1882, cyclone that traveled three hundred miles through Iowa "carrying destruction and death in its path" and another cyclone the following year that "wrecked 300 houses in Rochester, Minn., damaged 200 others, and killed twenty-five persons," doing $400,000 in damage. After citing other signs of the end, he concluded his appeal to all who would heed: "The great day of the Lord is truly near. . . . Let us give heed to the signs of the times fulfilling the prophetic word.' "

We've been waiting a long time for God to fulfill His promise to us, and many have begun to question whether it's ever going to be fulfilled. It's only natural that some Christians have decided that if they're ever going to have a heaven, they'll have to take matters into their own hands. So they begin to lay up treasures for themselves on earth and see to the inheritance of their children.

Fulfillment

Is God just testing our patience by putting off the Advent for so long? Not according to 2 Peter 3:9. Rather, the delay is part of His plan. It's actually *His* patience that's being tried, and He's exercising it by keeping the door of mercy open long enough for as many as possible to be saved.

WHY GOD WAITED

What about Abraham's case? Was God just delaying the birth of a son to test the old patriarch's patience? Not really. Once again, it was part of God's plan. Over and over again Abraham had to learn that it was not his own doing that brought the desired blessings into his life. And the same would be true when the son of promise was finally born. God waited until Sarah was too old to conceive and then made the impossible happen. That way Abraham could be proud of the son he had fathered, but he couldn't take credit for the accomplishment.

Was it just out of the sweetness of her heart that Sarah suggested to Abraham that he ought to take her handmaid Hagar as a concubine, or had he made her feel like an obstacle that was preventing him from accomplishing God's plan? Had he let slip a hint that "this whole childless thing can't be my fault, because God has promised children to me"?

Whether or not Sarah felt pressured to offer the Hagar solution, what she suggested was both legal and expected in the culture she came from. The laws stated that the maidservant of a woman could bear children for her mistress, and that legally the children would be considered as belonging to the mistress. So she gave Abraham his option. She stepped out of the way so that her man could prove himself able to do his part in seeing God's promises fulfilled.

And Abraham took her up on it. The temptation that came to him here was the same one he had faced in Egypt and at Gerar, only now it came under a different guise. Now he was not selling Sarah into slavery and going off to look for a better wife; he was merely setting her aside like a broken toy. He would still keep her and provide for her. In fact, according to law, she would still have first place among his wives.

When Abraham began sleeping with Hagar, the results were almost instantaneous. And they confirmed his suspicions about Sarah. Hagar had proven to Abraham that he was a real man. As for Hagar, as soon as she conceived she began to gloat. And Sarah ended up with less respect than her slave. Everyone knew now that the whole problem had been with Sarah all along.

The new gleam in Abraham's eye as he looked at Hagar, the new spring in his step, and the interest of all the household in the slave were too much for Sarah. The law would not allow her to send Hagar away, so she resorted to making life so miserable for her that Hagar finally fled.

It took an angel of the Lord to straighten out the mess and get Hagar back to Abraham's camp where she belonged. But it took a personal appearance by God to get Abraham's thinking straightened out.

So Hagar's child was born—and it was, oh praise God, a son! And God allowed Abraham to hope in this token of his own manliness, this symbol of his virility and ability to fulfill God's promise, for even longer than he had waited for his birth. Abraham named the boy *Ishmael*, "God hears," in honor of God's goodness to Hagar—and to him. Every time Sarah called the boy to dinner, the name reminded Abraham that he was an answer to prayer.

For thirteen years Abraham held Ishmael dear to his heart and repeated God's promises to him, reminding him over and over that God is faithful to His word and that *if we will just do our part*, He fulfills His promises every time. "God is going to bless us and bless all the world through you and me, Ishmael, because we've done our part in bringing you into the world!"

God let him believe that for thirteen years. Then He decided it was about time to go see His friend again and straighten out his theology— or at least tweak it a little more toward the truth.

---

[1]This quotation and those that follow are from J. G. Matteson's book *Prophecies of Jesus* (Battle Creek: Review and Herald, and Oakland: Pacific Press®, 1897), 158, 162, 164. Matteson died at the age of 60 or 61, a year before this book was published, without having seen his hope fulfilled.

CHAPTER THIRTEEN

Holiness

"When Abram was ninety-nine years old, the
LORD appeared to Abram and said to him, 'I am
Almighty God; walk before Me and be blameless.
And I will make My covenant between Me and
you, and will multiply you exceedingly.' Then
Abram fell on his face, and God talked with him,
saying: 'As for Me, behold, My covenant is with
you, and you shall be a father of many nations. No
longer shall your name be called Abram, but your
name shall be Abraham; for I have made you a father of many nations.'
"And God said to Abraham: 'As for you, you shall
keep My covenant, you and your descendants after
you throughout their generations. This is My covenant which you shall keep, between Me and you and
your descendants after you: Every male child among
you shall be circumcised' " (Genesis 17:1-5, 9, 10).

Abraham was approaching a century old and had been a wanderer
for God Most High for nearly a quarter of that time when God came to
see him again and put the kibosh on a big part of his theology—not for
the first time, but perhaps for the final time. At least, it doesn't seem
like God had to teach him this particular lesson again. The lesson was
that God prefers to bless us *apart from* our own efforts instead of *because*

of our own efforts. In short, God had to keep thwacking Abraham over the head with the lesson that the adage "God helps them that help themselves" isn't in the Bible and never will be.

Genesis 17 says that God came and introduced Himself by a new name: "God Almighty," *El Shaddai.* And He told Abraham what He expected of him—just one simple thing: "Walk before me and be blameless."

Which makes Abraham fall on his face.

To father a son is one thing. To walk blamelessly is quite another. Suddenly the man who has walked so proudly for the past fourteen years is powerless before his God. How can anyone set the bar that high? Perfection is a divine attribute, not a human one. Abraham knows he can't fulfill this latest requirement of God.

If he had picked up any elements of Egyptian theology while he was on his little detour down there, he knew that the pharaoh's priests had specific formulas that a person had to learn in order to be able to prove his or her blamelessness to the judging gods after death. By memorizing the right answers to forty-two questions, you could dupe the gods into thinking you'd lived a perfect life.

But Abraham had noticed that this God he was dealing with wasn't very dupable. You could make up whatever kind of stories you wanted to about yourself, but God would know the truth. And the truth was that Abraham couldn't figure out a way to live blamelessly. He'd messed up plenty of times already.

Abraham's prostration before God was one more indication that he was growing. The Mesopotamian religion of his day had no clear concept of guilt. Man's interaction with the divine was completely at the whim of the gods. In the hymn about the fall of Ur that I mentioned in chapter two, the author does not lament over the sins of the people and lay the blame to their account. Rather, the destruction of Ur results from an administrative decision made in the council of the gods, and it can't be overturned by any action of the people involved or even of the city's patron deities. Neither good nor bad behavior is rewarded by the gods; consequently, the gods have no particular expectations of righteousness on the part of humans.

El Shaddai, on the other hand, expects blamelessness.

But there's hope here, too. Up to now, God has been identified mainly as God Most High, a title denoting His rank. Now He comes with a name that expresses His power—because He wants Abraham to think in terms not of rank, but of empowerment.

As El Shaddai, God asks for the ultimate: blamelessness. It was too much for Abraham, and he knew it. All he could do was fall down and play dead—which was the response God expected from him. And when God had Abraham down and dead, He repeated His covenant and made it even stronger. He changed Abraham's name from *Abram,* "exalted father," to *Abraham,* "father of a multitude." And He began to speak in the future tense of how He would make Abraham exceedingly fruitful.

I can almost hear Abraham thinking, while he was down there on the ground, *But God, I've already been fruitful for You. I've produced the son I needed all along. Why all this talk about making me fruitful in the future? I've done just fine at being fruitful already.*

God didn't answer Abraham's thoughts just then but went on to talk about the covenant He'd made—saying that He would (in the future) establish, or make stand firm, the covenant. But first there was something He wanted Abraham to do.

FAITH ALONE

The previous covenantal encounter was one-sided, and purposely so. God bound Himself to be faithful unto death to supply descendants to Abraham. The patriarch had no part in making that covenant because God wanted him to know that the only thing required of him for the covenant to be fulfilled was for him to trust God to fulfill it. And when Abraham expressed his trust, God credited that faith to him as righteousness.

Then, despite God's care to make it plain that Abraham didn't have to do anything except trust, Abraham had set out almost immediately to do his part by having sex with Hagar. In a sense he broke the covenant then, because by taking things into his own hands, he abandoned his place outside the rows of animal parts and put himself in the middle with God—working together with God to produce the needed son.

When Abraham abandoned trust in favor of behavior, he abandoned the righteousness given to him because of his faith and chose behavior-based righteousness. How appropriate then for God to come back to him, after letting him try it his way for fourteen years, and remind him of what he really needed to have a successful walk with God. Righteousness.

When Abraham had admitted his inability to fulfill God's requirement, God gave him a second chance at the covenant. And this time he would have a part in it. This time he would bind himself by the shedding of blood. This time he would stake his life to faithfulness.

With Abraham still face down on the ground, dirty and unkempt before the Almighty, God revealed the terms of the covenant. He would do the blessing. Abraham would do the surrendering.

God said, in a sense, "Let's talk about how this covenant is going to be fulfilled. You, Abraham, think it's going to be fulfilled by the powers of your male member. But I say no, your virility will not accomplish anything at all. I, and I alone, will give you a son, just as I, and I, alone have the power to give you righteousness.

"You've lived nearly a century, Abraham, yet it doesn't seem that you've learned what I've been trying to teach you. You're still offering Me your strength to do My work. But what I really want is your weakness, and I want you to give it to Me by depending totally on Me instead of on yourself. As a symbol of your surrendering your strength to Me, I'm going to ask you to enter into the covenant with Me by giving Me the very thing you have been relying on to fulfill My purpose. Abraham, I want you to cut off the foreskin of your reproductive organ for Me. I want you to quit relying on it and start relying on Me.

"You will shed a little blood and experience a bit of pain in the process, and that will bind you to this covenant by your very life. It will bind you to trust Me instead of yourself for the rest of your life."

How easy it is to give God our strength to fulfill His will—to offer Him our talents, expertise, and learning and say, "Thank You for the abilities You've given me, oh Lord. Use them to Your glory." And then we go out and use those talents in the way that seems best to us and claim we are doing it for God's glory. All the while, however, we're watching out for the real Number One, making sure that we get proper credit for what we've done. How easy it is to give God our strengths. But how difficult to give Him our weakness. We don't like to feel like charity cases, and we don't like to feel like we owe anybody anything. We want to feel like we're pulling our weight.

One day I almost drowned off the coast of Hawaii. I'd been having great fun playing in the huge waves that were rolling in. Showing them I was so strong that they couldn't bowl me over. Posing for pictures and pretending I was omnipotent. Invincible.

Then one of them dragged me out into its element—the deep. I swam for shore with all my might, but another wave washed over me and sucked me farther out. *All right, if that's the way you're going to be, I can play that game too,* I thought. And I waited for another big wave and tried to ride its crest to shore. But it turned me in somersaults and pushed me toward nearby rocky cliffs. I came up spluttering and gasping for air, struggling now to stay on top.

The next wave did the same, and when I came up I knew I was a goner if another one got me. I started to wave frantically toward the shore and call for help. And then a boogie boarder who'd been watching my struggle came to my aid. He gave me his board, and together we went to shore.

I sat exhausted on the beach, draining water from my sinuses. I was embarrassed and ashamed that I had let something as small as the Pacific Ocean nearly kill me. I didn't feel very strong anymore. My omnipotence had been somersaulted into oblivion in front of a whole crowd of onlookers.

After a little rest, my wife and I made our way to our rental car. As we got in, she pointed to a man walking toward a car fifty yards away. "That's the man who saved you," she said. It had all happened so fast that I hadn't really seen who had done the good deed. I'd said a quick "Thanks" to him, but he had quickly disappeared into the surf after making sure I was safely on terra firma.

JOURNEY TO MORIAH

I knew that I should run over to him and thank him profusely now. But did I? I'm ashamed to admit it, but I actually shrank down into my seat, hoping he wouldn't see me. To go and thank him for saving me would be to admit that I had needed saving. That I had done something stupid and shown my weakness. That I had been powerless to save myself. So I let him get into his car and drive away without so much as waving at him.

Oh, the awesome power of the male ego!

Abraham had an ego too. He spent ninety-nine years trying to strike a decent bargain with God whereby he could contribute something to the deal and feel a sense of power and accomplishment. And all the while God was waiting for him to discover his weakness and to admit that he was powerless to meet God's requirements. When he finally did that, God changed his name to Abraham and for the first time let him play a part in their covenant.

In later years, circumcision came to be viewed as a work of the hands that automatically made a boy a part of God's chosen race. For Abraham it was nothing of the sort. In fact, it was just the opposite. It was a symbol of his utter inability to produce offspring who would be God's chosen race. It was a symbol of his surrender and total dependence upon God. At last he was giving up trying to make babies for God and was willing to let God work things out through His power.

Abraham didn't give up without a struggle. At one point in the discussion he pled for Ishmael, that God might allow this precious son to be the heir of promise. But God said, "No, I'm renaming Sarai *Sarah,* which means princess, because she is to be the mother of the promised son."

Abraham fell on his face again at that suggestion—to laugh, not to admit his helplessness. But God was firm in His purpose, just as He had been since the day He first called. Sarah would be the mother, and Isaac—the name means "he laughs"—would be her son. And this laughable event would all come about within a year's time.

CHAPTER FOURTEEN

Conversation

"The LORD appeared to him by the terebinth trees of Mamre, as he was sitting in the tent door in the heat of the day. So he lifted his eyes and looked, and behold, three men were standing by him; and when he saw them, he ran from the tent door to meet them, and bowed himself to the ground, and said, 'My Lord, if I have now found favor in Your sight, do not pass on by Your servant. Please let a little water be brought, and wash your feet, and rest yourselves under the tree' " (Genesis 18:1-4).

I spotted the men on my first trip around the track at the local high school. I was in a big hurry, jogging as fast as I could, making sure I kept my heart rate up to aerobic training level. Next time around, there they were again. And the next time too. They were making it about a third of the way around the track in the time it was taking me to complete the trip.

Conversing. That's what they were doing. And it intrigued me. In a language with peculiar rhythms that seemed to require considerable use of the hands, they were talking to each other. And talking and talking and talking. It seemed odd to me. What would two men have to say to each other that would take so long to say?

When I talk to another man, it's usually to convey some important information. Have you noticed that about American men? Most of us dislike telephones, for example, because conversation doesn't come naturally to us. I believe it was the president of the Western Union Telegraph Company who responded to Alexander Graham Bell's invention of the telephone by saying that it was an interesting thing, but he couldn't imagine what practical use it could possibly have—who would ever want to talk to someone far away? To his way of thinking, a telegraph with ten or fifteen carefully selected words ought to be sufficient to convey anything that couldn't wait for the post office's services.

Despite the proliferation of phones, American men's attitudes aren't much different than that today. Hand us a phone and tell us we need to call and talk to Grandma, and we're likely to ring her up and inquire about her health, relay information about how our kids are doing in school and what we're going to do for vacation next summer, find out how her replaced hip is feeling and what the doctor said about her gallstones, exchange a few pleasantries, and then hang up. It can all be done in seven to ten minutes max. Conversation for American men is about information. So, I just couldn't figure out what kind of information those two men had that would take so long to convey to each other.

Since then I've had opportunities to travel overseas and learn that the American way is not the only way. Particularly in Mediterranean cultures, I've seen men sit together or walk together and talk to each other apparently just for the sake of conversation. Sharing ideas; sharing themselves. Really getting acquainted with each other and establishing friendships based on mutual openness and caring.

I once took a research methods class at Georgetown University. Members of the class represented a cross-cultural amalgam; I think we had every habitable continent except Australia represented. When we discussed telephone interviews, several of the foreign students expressed their dismay at Americans' way of using the phone. In many countries, a telephone call is treated like a visit to the family home. You don't just launch into business matters. Other things must be discussed first: the family, health status, how things are going on the job, mutual friends, and then finally you come around, in an offhanded, back-door way, to the issue you really want to tend to. Here in America we have no time for such things. We call, get right down to business, and hang up. It seems that we hardly know how to carry on a conversation.

How does this propensity for information-centered interactions affect our relationship to God? What does fellowshipping with Him really mean? I think Abraham found the answers to those questions the day God found him sitting under a shade tree.

TIME FOR GOD

I've always had a hard time sitting still unless I'm doing something—reading a book or writing or researching something at the computer. When I was a young pastor, I would never sit out on the front porch or even in the backyard and just relax for fear of what people would think if they saw me doing nothing. Then one day, reading about Abraham, I discovered that the patriarch's longest recorded visit with God took place on a day when God found him sitting under a shade tree. Hmmm . . . Maybe God would like me to slow down enough for Him to catch up with me once in a while, too!

There Abraham sat in the heat of a summer day, relaxing under one of those great terebinths of Mamre. Whether or not he immediately recognized the three men who stood in front of him is not clear from the story, but he instantly leaped to his feet, ran to greet them, and offered his shady spot as a resting place. Then, running to the tent and to the herd, he set his whole household staff to work preparing a meal that would be remembered for millennia. The amount of flour he had Sarah prepare would easily make thirty loaves of bread of the size we make today—which means it would have made a lot more of the small loaves Sarah baked. And he had a whole calf prepared for meat. All for three guests. While his wife and servants worked to prepare the meal, Abraham no doubt played the role expected of a good host. He sat down to relax in friendly conversation with his guests. Whatever he thought of them at first, Abraham soon came to realize that these men were no ordinary travelers. They were God Himself and two angels come down in human form to visit with him and to check out the situation in Sodom and Gomorrah.

Playing the role of host, Abraham must have sat there and talked with them and listened and fellowshipped for several hours. Figure out how long it would take to roast an entire calf and bake enough bread to feed a small army, and you'll have a pretty good idea how long Abraham spent visiting with God that day. What a fantastic opportunity!

What do you suppose they talked about? Do you think Abraham brought up the whole "where's my heirs" issue again? Probably not. He did have Ishmael, after all, and God had just recently promised a son by Sarah. Besides, it wouldn't be proper to turn a social visit into a time for transacting business, unless the unexpected guests did it themselves. Abraham would be expected to keep the conversation light and personal, not heavy with demands or questions of justice.

When the food was ready, Abraham stood respectfully beside his guests while they ate, playing waiter, inquiring all along if everything was OK and whether he could get them a little more curdled camel milk or anything. It was during the meal that God repeated his promise to Abraham. "I'll be back next spring," God said. "And at that time Sarah will have a son."

Abraham listened in wonder, but this time he didn't laugh. He had spent the hours talking with God. He knew his guest too well to laugh at Him. Knew Him on a deeper level now—their relationship had been strengthened by time spent together.

How often do we hurry through our prayers as though the One to whom we're talking isn't worthy of any serious time? Prayer time is preciously short, so we need to get our list of wishes and intercessions conveyed efficiently. And there's even less time for listening to God speak to us.

Trouble is you can't get to really know someone when you're in that much of a hurry.

Under the shade tree Abraham had time for God. By this time he was ready for an in-depth encounter with God, not just to learn facts about Him or to hear His promises. Maybe the birth of Ishmael helped him slow down and take more time with God. Raising kids is enough to drive almost anyone to their knees at times! I can picture Abraham spending many hours in prayer for his son, talking to God about how he could help this half-Egyptian boy tame his naturally boisterous temperament and learn to have time for God.

A successful spiritual journey requires good conversation. Abraham's talk with God would continue even after the meal was done. Conversation on a very serious, life-and-death level. But before they got to that, there was time for one of the most important aspects of human communication: laughter.

CHAPTER FIFTEEN

Laughter

"Abraham fell on his face and laughed, and said in his heart, 'Shall a child be born to a man who is one hundred years old? And shall Sarah, who is ninety years old, bear a child?' And Abraham said to God, 'Oh, that Ishmael might live before You!'
"Then God said: 'No, Sarah your wife shall bear you a son, and you shall call his name Isaac; I will establish My covenant with him for an everlasting covenant, and with his descendants after him.' " . . .
"Then they said to him, 'Where is Sarah your wife?'
"And he said, 'Here, in the tent.'
"And He said, 'I will certainly return to you according to the time of life, and behold, Sarah your wife shall have a son.' And Sarah was listening in the tent door which was behind him. Now Abraham and Sarah were old, well advanced in age; and Sarah had passed the age of childbearing. Therefore Sarah laughed within herself, saying, 'After I have grown old, shall I have pleasure, my lord being old also?'
"And the LORD said to Abraham, 'Why did Sarah laugh, saying, "Shall I surely bear a child, since I am old?" Is anything too hard for the LORD? At the

appointed time I will return to you, according to the time of life, and Sarah shall have a son.'
"But Sarah denied it, saying, 'I did not laugh,' for she was afraid.
"And He said, 'No, but you did laugh!' " (Genesis 17:17-19; 18:9-15).

Scientists describe laughter as a "short exhalation of breath chopped into staccato segments lasting about one-fifteenth of a second each and spaced one-fifth of a second apart."[1] But they can't really explain it, at least not from an evolutionary standpoint. Laughter is a uniquely human talent. No other creature in the universe, as far as we know, can laugh—with the probable exception of God, in whose image we were made.

Anthropologists who travel the world studying humans and their customs and interactions tell us that they've never found a group of people who don't laugh. And as they've studied laughter, they've discovered that its most important purpose is to help establish social bonds. Because laughter is contagious, it brings people together—which is why speakers at conventions often begin their talks to groups who don't know them with a joke or two.

Imagine Abraham feeling comfortable laughing at something God said. I mean *really* laughing! Not chuckling. Not snickering. Laughing so hard he falls off his chair! (OK, he probably wasn't sitting on a chair, but I'm trying to paint a picture here! Wherever he started out, he ended up down on the ground, laughing.) You don't do that with someone you're scared of, do you?

In Genesis 15 we saw Abraham grow bold enough to call God up short on His promises, questioning His sincerity. That was a step forward in the relationship between the man and his superior. It demonstrated an acknowledgment of God as something more than a stop-and-go light. But he still wasn't on a deep friendship level with God.

Maybe you've had encounters with someone in authority over you whom you felt comfortable questioning or calling up short on her pronouncements. So you went into her office with fear and trembling, said your piece, accepted her response, and left—without ever laughing once.

That's a good relationship on one level. But wouldn't you rather have a boss with whom you could share a meal and conversation and even laughter? I would, because when you're both doubled over, guffawing, with tears running down your cheeks, you're on the same level. You've connected in a way that enables you to work together toward common goals. Your hearts are knit in a way nothing short of laughter can accomplish. I never feel as close to someone I can't laugh with as I do to someone who isn't afraid to join me in a good hoot.

GOD, LAUGHING

Now picture God's response when Abraham laughed so hard he fell on the ground. Does God take offense? Does He back away, looking confused and offended that His friend would find His promise so funny? No.

Do you know how I see this scene? Laughter is contagious, so I see God watching Abraham as he begins to chuckle at first, perhaps trying to stifle the laugh. But Abraham fails in this, then begins to laugh right out loud, bends over, slaps his knee, and then gives in to uncontrollable howls of glee and falls right down on his face. And to me, God doesn't look at all offended. In fact, as He watches Abraham, a smile begins to play at the corners of His mouth. Then He breaks into a big grin, and finally He starts to laugh too!

As Abraham regains his breath, he's thinking, *"Shall a child be born to a man who is one hundred years old? And shall Sarah, who is ninety years old, bear a child?"* (Genesis 17:17). Then the laughter gets the best of him again for a moment, and when he regains his composure, he says, "Oh, that Ishmael might live before you!" (verse 18). He's wiping tears from the corners of his eyes and streaks of mud off his cheeks as he says this, and God looks at him and can't help Himself.

"No," He says, His breath punctuated into those short, staccato segments. "Sarah your wife shall bear you a son, and you will name him . . ." And here God pauses and lets the laughter get the best of Him again for a moment. "You'll name him—get this—'He Laughs'! Get it?

JOURNEY TO MORIAH

You'll name your son 'He Laughs'! I don't want you ever to forget this joyful moment we've shared together, Abraham. Every time you look at your son. Every time you call him to dinner, I want you to remember this time when you and I laughed together!"

Wow! What a bond the man and his God shared at that moment! No wonder Abraham felt comfortable inviting God to stay for dinner when he saw Him and His two traveling companions a few days or weeks later. And as they sat around visiting after dinner, the topic of the son who soon would be born to Sarah came up again. "I'll be back next spring," God said. "I'll be here when Sarah gives birth to her little boy."

Sarah was eavesdropping from inside the tent, and God's words got the best of her. *How funny!* she must have thought. *This God who's been promising sons to Abraham ever since before we left Haran is promising one to me now, too! Ha! What a laugh! I went through menopause years ago.*

Sarah tries to stifle her laughter—don't you dare let God hear you laughing at Him—but she can't hold it in well enough for God not to notice. Does He get offended? Does He put His napkin to His lips and dab at them, a look of alarm in His eyes, glancing toward the tent door and raising His eyebrows to let Abraham know that he'd better have a little talk with this woman who dares to laugh at God's promises?

I don't think so. I see a twinkle in God's eyes as He looks at Abraham, because these two have shared laughter before. I see God's eyebrows go up, but His face bears a conspiratorial expression as He draws Abraham into the little bit of fun He's about to have with Sarah.

Abraham looks toward the tent door with alarm at first but then realizes that God's not upset. In fact He's planning to keep the laughter coming if He can. And now that Abraham's on the same page with Him, God speaks up. "What's up with Sarah laughing at Me?" He asks. "Does she think I can't do this? I've promised it, and it's going to happen!"

Then the man and his God wait to see how Sarah will respond. Will she come out with fear and trembling, apologize for laughing, and bow before God, pleading for mercy? Will she come out covering her mouth and tittering, apologizing lightly, "Excuse me—I'm sorry. It just sounded so funny to me! I didn't mean to laugh at You, though!" Or will she try to justify herself: "I'm sorry God, but what You say really is funny. I mean You promised Abraham here a son for something like a dozen years before You finally delivered one. What's to make me think You're any more serious about giving me a son by next spring? I mean, after all, I am a little beyond that, don't You think?"

Sarah chooses none of the above—because she's afraid of God. She won't challenge Him as Abraham did (Genesis 15). And she won't laugh with Him as Abraham did (Genesis 17). She just says, "I didn't laugh." She gives kind of a "Who me, laugh at You, God?" response because she hasn't gotten to know God as well as her husband has. Sarah has relied on second-hand information about this Deity who's chosen her family for special blessings.

At this point I can picture God looking at Abraham with a knowing smile and winking. Then He lowers His voice a note or two to sound more serious, all the while letting Abraham see the twinkle in His eyes. "No, but you did laugh," He says, letting Sarah know she's been exposed. But there's no condemnation in what He says, maybe just a hint of disappointment that she didn't 'fess up.

Just imagine though, what would have happened if she'd come out of the tent giggling. She and God could have had a rollicking good time laughing together about the wonderful news He'd brought. But she missed out because she was afraid to laugh with God.

How about you? Has your spiritual journey brought you to the place where you can have fun with God? Has the Sabbath—the day He wants to fellowship most closely with you—become a delight because of who you spend it with? That's what He wants to happen, according to Isaiah 58:13. He's the One who created us in His image—with the ability to laugh.

Have you shared a good guffaw with Him lately, or is your friendship not that close yet? If not, I hope you will soon, because Abraham's about to kick his relationship to the Almighty up another notch, and we're going along for the trip.

---

1. Sharon Begley, "The Science of Laughs," *Newsweek*, October 9, 2000.

CHAPTER SIXTEEN

Intercession

"He said, 'Let not the Lord be angry, and I will
speak but once more: Suppose ten should be found
there?'
"And He said, 'I will not destroy it for the sake of
ten.' So the LORD went His way as soon as He
had finished speaking with Abraham; and Abraham
returned to his place" (Genesis 18:32, 33).

I almost decided to title this chapter "Bargaining" instead of "Intercession" because that's essentially what Abraham did—he bargained for
souls, the very souls he had risked his life to rescue a decade and a half
earlier. Interceding sounds better in a spiritual discussion, I suppose.
But Abraham was essentially bartering or bargaining with God to see
what he could get.

What did Abraham have to offer God in exchange for His agreeing
to spare Sodom if there were ten righteous people in it? God's reputation with Abraham. And what future generations would take away from
Abraham's story of walking with God.

I'm glad Abraham had arrived at the point in his relationship with
God where he felt comfortable speaking up about his concerns, aren't
you? The story of his bargaining for souls reveals a lot about the character of God. It also points us to another, higher, level that God encour-
ages us to attain in our walk with Him.

Close friends confide in one another. They don't exchange just essential information—facts and figures that help them work together toward some goal. They talk about themselves, their plans, their hopes and goals, and the difficult decisions they have to make. It's good to have a close friend you can talk to when you're faced with a dilemma or an unpleasant task—someone you can bounce ideas off and who will be willing to speak his or her mind honestly.

God found a friend like that in Abraham. Moslems, Christians, and Jews all know Abraham as the friend of God because God confided in Abraham. That's what encouraged Abraham to kick the relationship up another notch.

After enjoying a sumptuous meal under the shade tree, the Lord and His angel companions got up to go on down the road. I think I might have breathed a sigh of relief as I watched them walk away and then flopped down in nervous exhaustion when they were finally out of sight. But not Abraham. He wanted to prolong his encounter with God as long as possible, so as his guests headed down the road, he stuck right with them.

God could see that Abraham was a true kindred spirit who wanted to prolong the fellowship, and He opened His heart—because His heart was heavy. He had a task to perform, but not one to His liking. He had to go down and check out the situation in Sodom and Gomorrah. The extreme wickedness of those cities and the surrounding villages had become a byword in the land. If any place beckoned for the fiery justice of God, it was Sodom. But God was not ready to pass judgment until He had seen the place for Himself.

Some of the elements in this story seem curious to us today, with our concept of God being up in a place called heaven, perhaps millions of miles away, but able to look down and see everything happening on earth—omnipresent Himself and able to dispatch angels to rescue us in the blink of an eye if the road we're on suddenly turns to black ice and our car begins to spin uncontrollably toward an oncoming semi. But for the sake of the story, we need to temporarily get back into the participants' minds and try to see the world as they did.

Most of the ancients thought of God as living on top of some nearby mountain. Or they pictured Him as dwelling just above the overturned bowl that formed the sky and using the earth as a stool for His feet. In either case, He wasn't much higher than the tops of the clouds. In one sense they thought of God as living closer than we conceive, but in another sense farther away—something like a kind uncle who lives on the other side of town. He'll always be there for you in a spiritual sense, but it might take him a while to drive over with his tools when your sink backs up.

To that mindset it made sense to think of God as having to come down and walk the dusty roads to find out what was really happening in Sodom. The amazing thing is that God was willing to work within people's ideas about Himself. So He got down and dirty and walked and talked with Abraham on His way to Sodom.

Weighed down with the horrific prospect of destroying life, God opened His heart to Abraham and shared what He had heard and what He planned to do about it. Abraham had played the role of Sodom's savior years before, and now he became its intercessor. Notice that he didn't argue with God. He had tried arguing with God about Ishmael's status but hadn't found God to be pliable on that issue. So now he's willing to accept God's will, just not in a laissez faire way. He's not going to simply surrender and blame any catastrophe on the will of God.

Abraham interceded with God because he cared. He had learned that God cares about people too, so his intercession wasn't a matter of arguing with God, but rather an attempt to better understand his Friend—to get inside His mind and clarify what God was thinking and planning. Getting inside the mind of God is one of the highest forms of worship.

PROBING GOD'S MIND

Abraham probed and questioned in his quest to know God. "Would you destroy the righteous with the wicked?" he asked. "What if there are fifty righteous people in the city? Would You still destroy it?"

Abraham knew about Sodom. He knew there wes serious sin in that camp. He had met its inhabitants and probably had a pretty good idea of how many of them really were righteous. So, after getting God to agree to save it for the sake of fifty, he started moving downward: "What if there are only forty-five?" "Well, how about forty?" "Thirty?" "Don't get mad now, God, but what if there are only twenty?" "All right, one last question (and it really will be my last one this time): What if there are only ten righteous people?"

And God plays along with him. He doesn't get upset. In fact, I can see God smiling as He goes through the bargaining session with Abraham, can't you? Smiling because He sees how kind and compassionate His friend is. Smiling because He sees a man who feels comfortable wrestling with God for the salvation of souls. And smiling because Abraham has grown past the self-righteous attitude that can't wait to see the wicked punished for their sins.

Self-righteousness looks around at others, sees their faults, and hopes they will reap their just reward. Self-righteousness is concerned only for its own salvation and becomes angry at the thought of less-righteous people, or people who have no concern for righteousness at all, receiving God's blessings.

When we have tried hard to be "good" and to maintain a close relationship with God, it's easy to fall into the trap of looking around at those who live only for pleasure and labeling them part of an "evil empire" fit only for the fire of God's justice. Abraham might have felt that way earlier in his life when he was trying by his own efforts to establish his own family and descendants. At that time the destruction of the cities of the plain might have looked like a blessing to him—good riddance of bad rubbish, an opportunity he could capitalize on. Proud of his own righteousness, he could have considered it God's way of clearing the valley of useless, sin-sotted trash so he could expand his holdings. But that would be self righteousness, and Abraham had moved beyond that. Contact with the mind of God had expanded his worldview to the point where he was interested in more than just his own welfare.

Self-righteousness wants evil wiped out as a justification of its own righteousness. Self-righteousness calls for the enforcement of strict justice because a self-righteous person expects to benefit from such justice—to be rewarded for his or her goodness at the expense of the not-so-righteous. But a mind tempered through contact with the grace of

God doesn't see things in quite such black-and-white terms. Abraham had experienced God's goodness to him in spite of his own badness, and that had changed his attitude toward other bad people.

So now as he walked down the road toward Sodom with God, he must have sensed the weight of the decision that God had to make. The fact that God would not just reach down and wipe out the Sodomites for their wickedness without coming down to see whether they could yet be saved showed that He was deeply concerned. Abraham sensed this concern and found that it matched his own feelings. And now he wanted to know just how concerned God was. What was His attitude toward the righteous, the wicked, and ultimate justice? Would He indeed destroy a city if a sizable minority of its inhabitants were righteous?

Abraham started out big—he didn't want to set the number too low and miss finding the answer to his question about God's character. He could have started out by asking if God would spare the city for the sake of ten. But if he had started there and gotten a "no" answer, he would never have found out what he really wanted to know: Would God spare a city for the sake of a sizable righteous population? Did He have no concern for the minority?

When he learned that God was concerned for the minority, he kept shrinking the number until he found out that God would indeed spare Sodom if there were only ten righteous people in it.

Would God have gone down to five? We'll never know because Abraham didn't ask. Maybe he felt secure in the number ten. Maybe he thought that all of Lot's family and a few of their close friends could be classified as righteous.

I'm glad Abraham pursued the question as far as ten, though, because his courage sets an example that can help us be courageous in our walk with God.

CHAPTER SEVENTEEN

Sodom

"The men said to Lot, 'Have you anyone else here?
Son-in-law, your sons, your daughters, and whom-
ever you have in the city—take them out of this
place! For we will destroy this place, because the
outcry against them has grown great before the face
of the LORD, and the LORD has sent us to destroy
it.'
"So Lot went out and spoke to his sons-in-law, who
had married his daughters, and said, 'Get up, get
out of this place; for the LORD will destroy this
city!' But to his sons-in-law he seemed to be joking.
"When the morning dawned, the angels urged Lot
to hurry, saying, 'Arise, take your wife and your
two daughters who are here, lest you be consumed in
the punishment of the city.' And while he lingered,
the men took hold of his hand, his wife's hand, and
the hands of his two daughters, the LORD being
merciful to him, and they brought him out and set
him outside the city" (Genesis 19:12-16).

Some scholars think the story of the angels' visit to Sodom and the
destruction of the cities of the plain doesn't even belong in the story of
Abraham. Our hero gets mentioned only once in it—as the one for
whose sake God spared Lot's life. But I think you'll agree—after we take

a closer look—that this story fits like a center puzzle piece in the story of Abraham's spiritual journey. To see just how it fits, however, we may have to get beyond some preconceived ideas of what the story is about.

Despite the way it's usually handled, it really isn't a "crime doesn't pay" story. Nor is it a story about a God who hates perverts. (Let's get another thing straight here—the sin of the men of Sodom has almost nothing to do with homosexuality. Every man in the town shows up, hoping to get a chance to abuse the handsome strangers. I doubt the whole town was made up of nothing but homosexuals—such a town wouldn't last for many generations, would it? No, the men outside the door are just men who want to party at someone else's expense. In the ancient world, heterosexual men often indulged in sexual encounters with other men purely for mutual pleasure or for their own pleasure if they could capture another man and force themselves upon him. Most civilizations in Abraham's day had no strictures against this. Don't misunderstand. I'm not justifying what they did—it was sinful. But I'm convinced their lascivious behavior was not the final factor in bringing destruction on their city.

On one level, the story is about the importance of hospitality—it comes just after the story of Abraham entertaining God and angels, and Lot wouldn't have been saved if it hadn't been for his hospitality. But that's not the main point of the story either.

The main point of the story is revealed in what happens after the angels strike their would-be attackers blind. That's when the Abraham call goes out to all of Lot's family. Remember, the whole story of Abraham is a story about a man who hears the call of God to leave his city, his family, and everything else behind and set out to follow God. That's exactly what the angels urged Lot to do, and Lot passed the call on to his extended family. But no one paid much attention.

Laughter comes up here too, in relation to God's message. When Lot appeals to his sons-in-law to do the Abraham thing—that is "get up and get out of this place" in response to God's call—they think it's all a big joke. "He seemed to be joking," the New King James Version says. But the word translated "joking" is the same word that's translated laughter in the earlier stories about Abraham and Sarah. It's the same root word that appears in Isaac's name. But this laughter at God is far different from Abraham's or Sarah's. The future parents of Isaac found God's words funny at first—but in the end they trusted what God had said. Lot's sons-in-law didn't, and they suffered the consequences.

Those consequences didn't come about because of the bad behavior on the front porch. They came about because the people of Sodom weren't willing to be like Abraham in following God. The people of Sodom weren't destroyed because of their sexual appetites or their lack of hospitality (although those sinful attitudes were no doubt factors in bringing the angels down on their inspection tour in the first place). They were destroyed because when God called them to trust Him and leave their homes, they answered with derision instead of faith. As a result they got destruction instead of deliverance.

A millennium later, a prophet named Jonah approached the wicked city of Nineveh with a message just like Lot's when the people repented in response to God's final appeal, God spared their city. But when Lot brought the warning and appeal to the Sodomites closest to him—the ones who'd had the greatest opportunity to develop a trust relationship with him and through him with God—they laughed him to scorn. That's why Sodom was destroyed: because not enough of the people had learned the lesson Abraham's story teaches, which is that trusting God enough to follow Him is the most important thing you can do. There were no spiritual pilgrims in Sodom. The city that needed at least ten adventurers for God ended up with only four—and they weren't really all that adventurous. The only reason they got out of the city was because "God remembered Abraham" (Genesis 19:29).

Abraham had it all arranged with God, and the angels were being true to God's promise when they gave Lot the opportunity to round up all those in the city who would believe God and respond to His call to leave the city. He needed to find only six in addition to his wife and daughters to make up the required ten believers whose obedience could spare Sodom. Unfortunately for the city, there were only four people the angels could even drag bodily out through the gates.

The story of Sodom and Gomorrah is often told as a story about God's justice and vengeance. But it's really a story about His mercy:

how hard He tries to save people. Lot and his wife and daughters were in no hurry to be saved. They were fooling around the house, packing their suitcases or whatever—maybe putting on their makeup, who knows—until almost dawn. Meanwhile the angels were pacing back and forth, reminding them that the whole place was about to go up in flames. Lot's family never did respond with a faith commitment to follow God—they didn't move until the angels grabbed them by the hands and led them step by step out of the city.

God seldom uses force to get people to follow. It was only His close friendship with Abraham that brought Him to it this time. And in all honesty, His mercy didn't pay very rich dividends, because the four people the angels rescued were no scions of righteousness.

Mrs. Lot hardly made it past the city gate because she'd left her heart in Sodom. Lot went out whining and complaining and begging to be allowed to live in a nearby small town, thereby saving it from destruction. But he soon learned that his whining hadn't really gotten him what he wanted. Zoar wasn't any better than Sodom, so he ended up having to flee from there too, without an angel escort this time. And the daughters? Well, they're credited with becoming the mothers, by incest, of two of the nations that became Israel's enemies a few centuries later.

There's a powerful message about God's mercy in this story of judgment. In it we see an amazing aspect of His character: For the sake of His friendship with Abraham, He behaves mercifully toward Lot, even though He knows it will cause problems down the pike.

The story of Sodom helps us understand the mind of God, because it lets us see Him struggling with a dilemma; playing off His desire to be merciful against the need for occasional demonstrations of justice; honoring friendship; doing everything He can to save people; making hard choices; exercising mercy even when it hurts. It lets us know that even God suffers in a world full of sin—that He can't always have things His way.

It's good that the story comes where it does, because in the upcoming chapters Abraham, too, will have to face painful choices.

CHAPTER EIGHTEEN

Sacrifice

"Sarah saw the son of Hagar the Egyptian, whom she had borne to Abraham, scoffing. Therefore she said to Abraham, 'Cast out this bondwoman and her son; for the son of this bondwoman shall not be heir with my son, namely with Isaac.' And the matter was very displeasing in Abraham's sight because of his son.
"But God said to Abraham, 'Do not let it be displeasing in your sight because of the lad or because of your bondwoman. Whatever Sarah has said to you, listen to her voice; for in Isaac your seed shall be called. Yet I will also make a nation of the son of the bondwoman, because he is your seed.'
"So Abraham rose early in the morning, and took bread and a skin of water; and putting it on her shoulder, he gave it and the boy to Hagar, and sent her away. Then she departed and wandered in the Wilderness of Beersheba" (Genesis 21:9-14).

When Isaac was born nine months or so after the Lord's shade-tree visit with Abraham, everyone rejoiced—except maybe Hagar. She had been barely tolerated by Sarah for the past fourteen years, tolerated only because she had provided the one thing Abraham needed most, a son. But now that Sarah had a son of her own, Hagar couldn't help wondering what this meant for her. If Sarah had been difficult before, what would she be now? And what would happen to her son, Ishmael?

We don't know, of course, exactly what legal system Abraham was operating under in his family relationships, but in some cultures from that era, a father was permitted to designate which of his sons was to receive the title and privileges of the firstborn. In other words, birth order didn't really matter. The birthright could be transferred from one son to another. And the father's word was final, even if he was tricked into blessing the wrong son. That seems to have been the case with Jacob and Esau later.

Hagar and Ishmael couldn't have helped overhearing the news about the wonderful promises God had made to Abraham concerning the son who was to be born to Sarah. So as soon as it was announced that Sarah's child was indeed a boy, Hagar must have known she was on shaky ground.

Sarah laughed and laughed and laughed when it was all over. "God has made me laugh," she said, "so that all who hear will laugh with me" (Genesis 21:6). She wanted everyone to share in her great joy. Everyone except Hagar and Ishmael, that is. She'd already driven Hagar away once with her cruel treatment, shortly after the poor girl got pregnant by Abraham. Now she looked at her handmaid with unbridled contempt.

Things continued on that rather rough footing for a couple of years, but then it came time to wean Isaac, and that occasioned a big party. Everyone was happy, laughing, having a great time, when suddenly the festivities were brought to an abrupt halt.

Sarah saw the son of Hagar the Egyptian, whom she had borne to Abraham, laughing. Therefore she said to Abraham, "Cast out this bondwoman and her son; for the son of this bondwoman shall not be heir with my son, namely with Isaac" (Genesis 21:9, 10, margin).

Someone was having entirely too much fun. It was sixteen-year-old Ishmael. Sarah saw him laughing. There was nothing wrong with that, was there? She had said everyone should laugh with her. But not Ishmael, I guess. He should be sitting off in a corner somewhere, feeling sorry for himself because he's no longer in first place around here. And so the party came to a screeching halt. It was crisis time for Abraham.

Sarah saw Ishmael as a threat to her son, so she demanded that Abraham send Hagar and Ishmael away. Abraham saw things differently. He had learned to accept the fact that Ishmael wasn't the promised seed as far as God was concerned. But he still loved his son and couldn't bear the thought of having to part with him. This was the boy he'd groomed as his heir for thirteen years! To send a son away goes against all the natural instincts of a father. No matter what conflict the child may cause, a father by nature wants to bind his family together. He would, if he could, stretch out one hand to each of the opposing parties and by the very strength of his own life pull them together or be torn apart trying.

But Sarah wouldn't hear of it. And God took Sarah's side! It wasn't punishment for Abraham's mistake in trying to supply his own son; it was just the painful result of his wrong move. Life is full of hard choices, God could say from long millennia of experience.

Judging from the laws of some of the cultures around Abraham, Sarah probably had no legal right to send her handmaid away. Only Abraham could do the deed. Now he had to pay the price for his mistake in trying to run ahead of God.

Abraham not only sent Ishmael away but also cut him off from the family inheritance—just as his own family had done to Aberham. Rising early in the morning, perhaps after struggling with God all night, Abraham sent Hagar and Ishmael off with nothing but a little bread and water for their journey.

Frankly I don't understand that. I mean, couldn't he have at least have provided a little better for them—given them a little bag of silver, saddled a couple of donkeys for them to ride, and sent along a goat or two to provide milk? There must have been a lot of vindictiveness on Sarah's part. Is that her we see there in the tent door as Abraham bids his son goodbye? Hands on her hips. Watching everything with eagle eyes to make sure Abraham doesn't slip his son an extra morsel.

Yet even in this seemingly heartless answer to a man grasping for consolation God communicated His special love for Abraham. Ishmael was the son of Abraham's mistake, the son of his self-dependence and self-righteousness. He represented the folly of trying to fulfill God's promises by human strength. If God were purely a God of justice, the boy ought to be abandoned with no hope. It would be a lesson for us—that there's no hope for us if we try to work out our own salvation apart from God.

WHY GOD BLESSED ISHMAEL

God had already predicted that this carnal son of Abraham would be a wild one—even before he was born. "He shall be a wild man; His hand shall be against every man, and every man's hand against him," said the angel who met pregnant Hagar in the wilderness when she fled from Sarah's cruelty (Genesis 16:12). So if he was going to be such a feral fellow, why would God want to have anything to do with him? Isn't God interested only in the people who will calmly and pliantly follow His leading?

The answer's the same as the answer to the question of why God rescued Lot from Sodom: God would bless Ishmael for Abraham's sake. God would not abandon Ishmael, because Abraham had pled for him when God first promised the birth of Isaac. "Oh, that Ishmael might live before You!" Abraham had said. And even though God denied his request that Ishmael be the official son of promise, there still was a promise or two He could give to Ishmael: "As for Ishmael, I have heard you. Behold, I have blessed him, and will make him fruitful, and will multiply him exceedingly. He shall beget twelve princes, and I will make him a great nation" (Genesis 17:20).

The promise seemed about to wither and die under a bush in the desert a few hours after Hagar left home with him. (Once again, there's something odd about the story here. I think it reveals a little about how these wonderful stories of Abraham and his kin have come down to us—not as official records of precisely what happened, but as good stories about events that happened, with a bit of the storyteller's embellishment here and there. Ishmael was about sixteen years old by now—

probably taller and stronger than his mother. But the story pictures him as if he's a little baby whom his mother could hide under a clump of sagebrush.)

This story tells us that God doesn't renege on His promises. Hagar may not be terribly well tuned in to His leading at this point. Her life has basically fallen apart. Both she and Ishmael are discouraged and ready to give up. But God is watching all this with interest, and when it seems that all is lost, an angel asks, "What ails you, Hagar?"

That's the way the New King James Version translates it, and I love it, because that's a phrase my mother would use kind of sarcastically. It was her way of saying "What's your problem?" when she thought the person shouldn't really be having a problem.

You see, there's a well just a few paces away, and God knows this. Hagar can't see it because she's allowed life to get her down to the point where she isn't even thinking straight anymore. But God has a solution to her problem whether or not she can see it. " 'Fear not,' " the voice says, " 'for God has heard the voice of the lad where he is. Arise, lift up the lad and hold him with your hand, for I will make him a great nation.' And God opened her eyes, and she saw a well of water. Then she went and filled the skin with water, and gave the lad a drink" (Genesis 21:17-19).

Her eyes weren't physically closed before the angels spoke—they just weren't spiritually open to see and trust God's leading. It's the words of God's promise that open her eyes to see the well of water.

That kind of thing happens often to spiritual pilgrims. Even though Abraham's pilgrimage wasn't Hagar's own, she, along with her son, reaped some of the benefits of her erstwhile lover's journey.

The well became a symbol of God's provision for Abraham's son in the wilderness. Remember in chapter six, when I suggested that you highlight all the occurrences of *see* and *appear?* Well, this is one of those places you ought to mark, because once again that important Hebrew word that means either *see* or *provide* shows up. In this trip to the wilderness, God opened Hagar's eyes to *see* a well. The time before, when she fled from Sarah while she was pregnant, Hagar had another *seeing* experience by a well and named the place Beer Lahai Roi—"Well of the

Living One Who Sees Me." In that encounter she called God *El-Roi*—"The God Who Sees." That could equally well be translated "The God Who Provides." There are many parallels between Hagar's experience in the wilderness with the near death of Ishmael and Abraham's later experience on Mt. Moriah and the near death of Isaac. In both instances, the parent comes to know the God who sees and provides, and the life of the boy is spared.

After hearing the voice of the angel of the Lord calling from heaven and seeing the well, Hagar abandoned her plan of going back to her home in Egypt. She found a wife for her son in her homeland, but Ishmael and his descendants lived and thrived in the harsh deserts of the Sinai Peninsula.

From Abraham's perspective, Ishmael's departure must have been a terrible test of his faith. Why would God ask this of him? It was as though his beloved son had to be made a living sacrifice—handed over to God, to let God take care of him from now on. And all Abraham could do was trust that God would make good on His promises.

As far as we know, Abraham never saw Ishmael again, but the son never forgot his father. When Aberham died more than seventy years later, Ishmael came back. And though Abraham had fathered and sent away other sons, it was the two favorite sons of the patriarch who joined together in burying him.

DETOUR TO BEERSHEBA

Abraham's life was full of the blessings of the Lord, but he also knew sacrifice. In fact his path, ever since he'd left Haran, had been a journey to a mountain where he would be called upon to make the ultimate sacrifice in order to demonstrate his faith in God. Before we get to that story, however, the Bible's storyteller takes us on what seems like a bit of a detour. At the end of Genesis 21, there's the story of Abraham, Abimelech, and the well of Beersheba. It's almost as though, after telling the story of Hagar and Ishmael wandering in the wilderness of Beersheba, Moses said "Oh, and speaking of Beersheba—let me tell you how that famous place got its name." The story's not a total excursus, though, because it reveals some significant information about just how much God had blessed Abraham in spite of the hard trial he had just been through in giving up his son.

The last part of Genesis 20 contains a story about Abimelech giving Abraham sheep, oxen, and money, plus permission to live wherever he wants on Abimelech's land. In chapter eight, I explained why I think this story belongs earlier in the chronology of Abraham's life. Nonetheless, looking at the structure of the story as it is told, it's significant that just before we hear about the birth of Isaac, Abimelech is the one in charge, giving gifts to Abraham. Then immediately after Isaac's birth and Ishmael's departure, Abimelech appears again, bringing his military commander with him. But this time he's singing a totally different tune: "I can see that God is with you in everything you do," he says to Abraham. Now, instead of beneficently granting Abraham permission to live on his land, Abimelech seeks reassurance that neither Abraham nor his descendants will turn on him and become his enemy.

There's no way the storyteller could have proclaimed more clearly: Abraham has arrived. Because of God's blessing he's no longer an alien dwelling on other people's land; he's a force to be reckoned with. And Abimelech's concern about his own posterity acknowledges that now, for the first time, he's concerned that Abraham's clan isn't a mere passing presence. It's clear to him that his descendants are going to have to deal with Isaac, and that his grandchildren will be dealing with Isaac's children, and so on.

Abraham is only too glad to make a covenant with Abimelech to keep their relationship on above-board terms. Abraham's headquarters is twenty miles from Abimelech's, but the two men's shepherds have been butting heads, fighting over a well in the wilderness, so Abraham brings up this point to Abimelech. "You want to keep our relationship on an honest basis," he says. "Well, what about that well your servants chased my servants away from?"

"*What?*" Abimelech responds. "I never heard a thing about that!"

Notice what happens next.

Abraham has brought sheep and oxen with him, and he proceeds to give some of them to Abimelech. Making a covenant requires a sacrifice. The fact that Abraham was the one to provide the animals for the sacrifice makes a highly significant statement about his status. In the previous chapter, Abimelech is the "big man" who can be beneficent with his little neighbor, giving him sheep and oxen. Now Abraham's the one bringing the gifts. And in a situation like this, a gift can be a demonstration of power. It says "I'm on my own now. I'm no longer dependent on your hospitality for survival in this land. In fact, I have more than enough. I can better afford to supply the animals for the covenant sacrifice than you can."

By accepting the gifts, Abimelech acknowledges Abraham's status as a peer, and the two men make mutual promises to stop fighting over territory. And after Abimelech heads back home, Abraham stays beside the well of Beersheba—the well of the covenant—and plants a tree. The tree, which will need water from the well, witnesses to the terms of the agreement. Abraham will continue to have access to the water.

It seems that nothing in this harsh land can be accomplished without hard work and sacrifice—literal sacrifice. But nothing could prepare Abraham for the next sacrifice that would be required of him.

Nothing, that is, except the years of journeying and training he'd undergone on his way to Mt. Moriah.

CHAPTER NINETEEN

The Journey

"It came to pass after these things that God tested
Abraham, and said to him, 'Abraham!'
"And he said, 'Here I am.'
"Then He said, 'Take now your son, your only
son Isaac, whom you love, and go to the land of
Moriah, and offer him there as a burnt offering on
one of the mountains of which I shall tell you.'
"So Abraham rose early in the morning and
saddled his donkey, and took two of his young men
with him, and Isaac his son; and he split the wood
for the burnt offering, and arose and went to the
place of which God had told him. Then on the
third day Abraham lifted his eyes and saw the place
afar off" (Genesis 22:1-4).

How did you get out of bed this morning, Abraham? How could
you get up early on a day like this?

What was running through your mind as you split the wood? Did
you wish you could take the axe to your own neck rather than face the
day? How long did you stand looking down at your son before you
awakened him and told him to prepare for a journey?

Why is there no argument with God now? You spoke up for Ishmael
when God took the covenant blessing away from him. Why won't you
at least try to defend this new son of yours?

JOURNEY TO MORIAH

And what do you think of your God now?

There are Canaanites living around you who sacrifice their first-born sons to their gods. Did you really think you'd found a better, kinder god? Well, what do you think now?

What's it all been about—this thirty-some-year journey following a God who promises descendants? What's been the point? Does He ever keep any of His promises? I mean, didn't He say that Isaac would be the one to father the multitude of descendants you're supposed to have? Now He's asking you to offer Isaac as a burnt offering.

Does any of your Mesopotamian background come back to you now? Do you remember any of what the priests there taught about the fate of a person whose body goes up in smoke? It's the worst possible fate, you know. If those priests are right, your sacrificed son won't have any future existence at all. He's just gone!

And what about yourself? If you have no descendants, who will provide for you in the next world? A man needs to have many sons to be sure there will be someone to bring offerings to the temple in his name.

(Please don't misunderstand—I'm not suggesting that Abraham necessarily believed everything the Mesopotamians taught about what happens when a person dies. But if he spent any time at all pondering his options, these sorts of questions could easily have arisen in his mind.)

And on an even more practical level: What about all your flocks and herds and other trappings of wealth—the things God has blessed you with? If you have no son to take care of these things after your passing, what will happen to them? What enduring testimony will there be to the life of a man who devoted himself to following God?

The most amazing thing to me about the story in Genesis 22 is that God's call to sacrifice Isaac doesn't appear to have been a crisis for Abraham at all. He seems to go through the motions of preparing for the sacrifice and making the journey as if he's in a trance. No emotion is betrayed. The man who laughed at God's proclamation that Isaac would be born and who pled face-in-the-dust for his son Ishmael doesn't seem to even wince at God's proclamation that Isaac must die a most horrible death.

The Journey

Is Abraham just numb? Does he feel like God has jerked him around so much already that there's no point in getting emotional about anything anymore?

Children of abusive alcoholic parents often retreat into a world devoid of expectations of weal or woe. Because their parents behave totally unpredictably, the children learn to separate themselves from their emotions to keep from being hurt. Is that what's happened to Abraham by this time? Has he had his hopes raised and dashed so many times that nothing matters to him anymore?

Actually, no. He's still full of expectations of good things from God. But we have to read farther into the story to discover what and why. Before we do that, let's consider what, exactly, God asked Abraham to do.

To Abraham, Isaac represents the one and only tangible evidence that the God he has followed is real and can be trusted. Abraham set out from Haran with nothing in his pocket but a promise from God. He waited eleven years before Ishmael's birth finally gave him some evidence that God planned to make good on that promise of descendants. Then, thirteen years later, God took that evidence away from him and replaced it with the promise that Sarah would bear Isaac. Three years or so after that, God took Ishmael completely out of his life and focused the spotlight of faith and evidence with laser precision on Isaac and Isaac alone.

For the past dozen or more years, Abraham's whole life and whole faith have centered on Isaac. All his joy has centered on the laughter God brought into his life. the journey has been long and difficult, but it seemed to be leading to a destination filled with joy and laughter.

Now this. Now God is telling him, "Take your faith—and the very reason for your faith. Lay it on the altar and burn it up. Leave no trace. Send it all winging heavenward toward Me."

What will you do when all the evidence on which you base your faith is gone? What did Abraham do when God asked him to destroy the evidence?

He set out to do it, without asking any questions.

Why?

The answer's there. Up on Mt. Moriah. But we can't find it unless we go there with him.

CHAPTER TWENTY

Moriah

"They came to the place of which God had told him. And Abraham built an altar there and placed the wood in order; and he bound Isaac his son and laid him on the altar, upon the wood. And Abraham stretched out his hand and took the knife to slay his son" (Genesis 22:9, 10).

A man stood on top of a mountain.

On top of a mountain, with no place to go but down.

One does not arrive on the top of a mountain by gliding gently down a stream on a lazy summer's day. Nor does one arrive at the top of a mountain while reclining on a couch in the comfort of the living room. Mountains must be climbed slowly, carefully, one step at a time.

Abraham had not arrived at the top of Mt. Moriah by taking the easy way. He had set out, forty or so years earlier, to answer the mysterious call of God. He had set out to walk by faith. Many times along the way his feet had faltered. But in every instance when he tried to go it alone, to solve his problems himself, or to help God along a little, he learned that he had been called to something higher: to total trust in God even when it seems as though there's no reason to trust.

And every time he put his hand in the hand of God and walked by faith, God blessed him. In fact, God even blessed him when he failed to walk by faith, and that taught him something about faith and about God that he couldn't have learned if he hadn't had those mission-critical failures.

God didn't allow Abraham to crash and burn even when he failed to tune in to His guidance system and tried to go it on his own, because Abraham was His friend, and God had a very special mission for him—Abraham's story was to teach us about faith.

There's a certain amount of idealism about the story. We don't get the whole story—only the high and low points. Obviously, a lot of other things happened to Abraham that we don't know anything about—no doubt other struggles of faith.

I've known of people who set out idealistically to follow a vision that they believed God had given them, who seemed to me to be way off course. On one hand I want to caution them that maybe this vision they've had isn't from God—maybe they ought to reconsider where they're headed and live life a little more "normally." But on the other hand, I have a feeling that if I had known Abraham, there would have been times—even when he was doing what turned out to be the right thing—when I would have given him the same counsel. How can I know what's right for someone else? I'm not sure I can.

My own spiritual journey has taken some twists and turns I never anticipated. And it goes on. Looking back, I can see how God has led through various circumstances, taking me from a place where I had decided He did not exist and giving me enough evidence that I was wrong to get me started on a life pursuing knowledge of Him. Revisiting what I had written about Abraham nearly twenty years ago, I discovered that my own conception of God and what it means to follow Him has changed drastically over the years. I no longer see the world through the same eyes I did then. Even the lessons I take away from Abraham's story are different. And I think that's a good thing. Because a spiritual journey is not a journey at all if you let it stagnate.

Maybe that's what was happening with Abraham by the time Isaac was sixteen or so years old. Having passed through many trials and come out with his faith intact and with the son of promise—son of faith—by his side, Abraham could easily have begun to think that he'd arrived. That he'd accomplished all the spiritual growing he needed to do. He was ready for retirement, don't you think? By the time he's one hundred oughtn't a man to be allowed to rest on his lees a bit?

But God had one more challenge for him. "Now that you've learned to live by faith in My promises and My provision, lay your faith on the altar." That was an extremely strange request from a God who had invested so much effort in teaching Abraham to have faith. His faith has born fruit. And now it was time to give the fruit back to God.

WHERE IS THE LAMB?

The man and his son climb the mountain, the son carrying the wood. And then the question. "Isaac spoke to Abraham his father and said, 'My father!' And he said, 'Here I am, my son.' And he said, 'Look, the fire and the wood, but where is the lamb for the burnt offering?'" (Genesis 22:7).

Isaac thinks his father is getting a little forgetful in his old age, and he just wants to help out. However, that's anything but the case. Abraham has thought of nothing else but the lamb for the offering all the three-day journey from home. And he has an answer: "My son, God will provide for Himself the lamb for a burnt offering" (Genesis 22:8).

If there's one tidbit of faith that Abraham wants his son to inherit, it's this: "God will provide." It's the lesson Abraham has had to learn all the way along on his journey. And looking back over that journey, he recognizes that all he has, including this son, is a direct result of God's providing. All his own attempts at doing the right thing have yielded no benefits to match the result of simply trusting God. Abraham hasn't spent his life on a couch, waiting for God to do everything. He's been active all along. But he knows that God's part has played the larger role in bringing about all the good things that have happened. Seventy-five years of sleeping with his beautiful wife produced zilch. But after all that time the promise of God produced a son. Now, after all that, how can Abraham argue with the evidence that "God will provide"?

This phrase is interesting and slightly enigmatic because it can mean either "God will provide" or "God will see." Pregnant Hagar had met the Lord as "the God who sees" when she fled from Sarah (Genesis

16:13). When she returned home, she must have told Abraham about "the God who sees," but he named her child "God will hear." Then, later, when Abraham sent Hagar and Ishmael away, God opened Hagar's eyes to see the well of water that spared their lives. It was clear to Abraham that his whole clan was learning to interact with the very personal seeing and hearing God whom he had followed out of Haran.

I suppose Abraham's answer to Isaac meant "God will see to it," or perhaps "God can already see the lamb." It was an expression of faith. Abraham knew what he would have to do when he got to the top of the mountain. But in spite of that, he knew in his heart that God would not stop providing just because the son He provided has to be sacrificed.

Was this blind faith on Abraham's part? A leap in the dark? Or was it trusting Someone you've learned through experience is trustworthy?

That's what his whole journey was about. And that's why the journey climaxes here. At the beginning of his journey, God promised to *show* him the land his descendants would possess. God has done that. Abraham has *seen* it. And God has also *shown* him the first of his descendants. Abraham now knows that his God can see the future. So why should he have to worry about it? Why argue? Why plead? It is action God has asked for, and action He will get.

So Abraham marches to the top of the mountain, perhaps not with *all* his questions answered, but with the necessary ones answered.

He slowly builds an altar—something he has done at each important stopping point along his way.

He lays the wood on the altar.

The Bible tells us nothing of any conversation that passed between father and son while all this was going on. It doesn't even explain how the old man persuaded his virile young son to submit to being bound and laid down to die.

Did it all pass in silence? Was Abraham too choked with emotion to speak; his son too wrapped in wonder to ask any further questions? Did all communication proceed with facial expressions and gestures while a sense of awe and foreboding descended on the place God had told

Abraham about and led him to? We don't know, because the only conversation recorded at this exclamation point of history is the conversation between the man and his God.

Abraham stands on top of the mountain with no place to go but down—unless he will look up. But he is looking down. Down at the literal embodiment of faith and promise. Down at the only tangible evidence of the value of faith. Down at the knife in his hand that must strike out at that one tangible thing.

He could choose to turn his back on the task at hand, untie the boy, and walk with him down to the bottom of the mountain. But as soon as he takes the boy by the hand and lifts him off the altar, his faith will have died. He will have ceased to follow the God he met first at Haran, and he will have begun to walk in his own strength again, adrift in a world with no meaningful faith.

To kill the boy would seem to be to destroy his faith. But he knows that to let the boy live when God has said he must kill him will destroy his faith. So he lifts his hand above his head, still looking down. And in the moment of silence before he strikes, he hears a voice from heaven. It's the Messenger of God calling! And he has a new message from God for God's friend: "Do not lay your hand on the lad, or do anything to him; for now I know that you fear God, seeing you have not withheld your son, your only son, from Me" (Genesis 22:12).

Abraham has done what needed to be done. He has demonstrated that his faith is in God, not in the things God provides. That though everything he treasures on earth should be taken away from him, he will still believe.

HARD QUESTIONS

One of the hardest things for unbelievers to understand about believers is why they continue to cling to faith in the face of the horrible realities of this world—a world filled with suffering and pain, where innocent children die by the thousands every day from starvation, malaria, AIDS, disasters, neglect, abuse, you name it. If there is a God in heaven, why aren't the innocent protected? Why aren't all believers blessed with riches like Abraham's? Why do those who pray suffer just as many losses as those who never give God a second thought?

Abraham on Mt. Moriah answers that question by saying that there is something more to life than what you can see and hold in your hands. What really counts is knowing that there is a God in heaven who does care, whether or not He can make the decisions we think He ought to. It's knowing that if you abandon your faith, you have abandoned everything that makes life worth living. That if you turn your back on your spiritual journey, you will cease to really live. That if you cease seeking the God who is higher than this world, you will have quit climbing and begun to slide down into the oblivion of the morass of things.

Abraham's relationship is with God, not with his son nor his flocks nor his tents. It is with the God who has called him and shown him the way all along. And while in some people's book that may make him "too heavenly minded to be of any earthly good," he has learned to live this way through years of experience, of trying to do it the other way.

This is a different Abraham from the man who left Haran. Different because of what he has experienced. Different because of the mistakes he has made. Different because of the times he has failed to have faith. Different because of the times he has walked by faith. Different because of the times he has ignored God. Different because of the times he has listened. Different because of the years that have passed and the things he has seen and the things he has done and the people he has met and the battles he has fought. But most of all, different because he has learned to have implicit, total, unquestioning faith that there is a God in heaven who cares about him and will work things out for him and his future, whether or not he has anything in his hands to prove it.

There is a creative tension in this belief. At the bottom of the mountain he told his servants, "Stay here with the donkey; the lad and I will go yonder and worship, and *we* will come back to you" (Genesis 22:5, emphasis supplied). At the top of the mountain he bound the boy and prepared him for death.

Abraham doesn't know how both things can be true: That he will sacrifice his son and that he and his son will come down the mountain together. He just knows that God has promised to provide for his future through this son, and there's no point in doubting God's word. And so he goes to the top of the mountain, intent on obeying God's command and leaving the results with God. Faith is sometimes like that. It says things that are hard to believe in the present circumstances.

That's real faith. But it's also scary faith, because we've all heard news stories about people who did strange and horrible things because they thought they heard the voice of God telling them to do it.

The difference between Abraham and the David Berkowitzes of the world is that Abraham had spent a lifetime learning to know the voice of God and seeing God bless him when he responded to it. He was not a schizophrenic with a chemical imbalance in his brain. He was a man who had put God to the test time after time, year after year, and learned to know the difference between impressions and messages. He had persevered in his journey for a long time, and the outcome was that he had a faith he knew he could rely on. Faith in a God he knew he could rely on—even if that God demanded strange things.

The walk to the top of Moriah was a continuation of the walk out of Haran. But Abraham could never have climbed Moriah the first time he passed it, on his way from Shechem to Egypt. God had led him through the experiences he needed in training for this marathon climb.

So, when Abraham arrives at the top of Moriah, he is about 115 years old—not a day too soon or too late; right on God's schedule. He's right across the valley from Melchizedek's home here, but he needs no priestly intercessor now. He and the Almighty are on personal terms. So when God's Messenger calls from heaven, Abraham, who has been looking down at the evidence for his faith, immediately looks up. "Abraham lifted his eyes and looked, and there behind him was a ram caught in a thicket by its horns. So Abraham went and took the ram, and offered it up for a burnt offering instead of his son" (Genesis 22:13).

There it is: evidence that he was right to have faith even when it seemed that following that faith would rip the last vestige of hope from his life. It's one of those *voilà!* moments, when the voice from heaven opens someone's eyes to see something that's been there all along. It's a real event that provides a powerful metaphor for us. God has already provided what we need, and it will become visible in His good time.

Abraham takes the ram and sacrifices it, then names the top of the mountain "The LORD Will Provide." Abraham knew that on the way up the mountain. He knows it with even more certainty now.

At one time I thought the point of the story of the binding of Isaac was that God is a taker, that He asks of us what we treasure most. But Abraham now knows that God is giver, not a taker—a point that would be driven home most powerfully nearly two millennia later by a Roman hammer and nails on this very same hill, where God "*gave* his only begotten Son that whosoever believeth in him should not perish, but have everlasting life" (John 3:16, KJV; emphasis supplied). Abraham has learned what he needed to learn, and now his son and he can go down the mountain together.

The rest of Abraham's life is little more than an addendum, even though he lives another sixty or so years. In those years he purchases a tiny parcel of the land God has promised to him and buries Sarah in it. He finds a suitable wife for Isaac and raises a whole 'nother family himself, but sends them all away from the land God has promised to the son of promise. Then, finally, he dies after spending a hundred years following God.

But the climax was on Mt. Moriah—where he demonstrated that he trusted God explicitly, implicitly, and totally. It's where he was going on his spiritual journey. And where he challenges you and me to go.

When Did
All This Happen?

It's actually possible to get a pretty good idea of when the events recounted in Abraham's story took place. The customs and actions described fit best into what archaeologists call the Middle Bronze Age— that is, sometime between 2200 and 1550 B.C.

The genealogical lists in Genesis can help us narrow down the range quite a bit, but they can't give us an exact year for Abraham's birth. Suffice it to say that he probably lived about as long before the birth of Christ as we are living after it. In a 1995 article in *Biblical Archaeology Review,* renowned Egyptologist Kenneth A. Kitchen defended the historicity of the stories of the patriarchs Abraham, Isaac, and Jacob, and suggested that they lived between 1950 and 1700 B.C. And the eminent archaeologist and chronologist Siegfried Horn also suggested that Abraham may have been born about 1950 B.C.

Personally, I like to have a little fun with this. Since I was born in A.D. 1951, why not use 1951 B.C. for the date of Abraham's birth? If you prefer 1950 or maybe the year you were born, fine; I won't argue with you! Whatever date you choose, just remember that the main parts of the story probably fit into the 1800s B.C.

We can't determine exactly when Abraham was born because biblical chronology before the time of King David involves a lot of variables, and dates can't be pinned down precisely. But archaeological finds and written records from the nineteenth century B.C. confirm that era was a time when a man like Abraham could have made the journey he did, formed the type of alliances he had in Canaan, and practiced the lifestyle described in his story.

When Did All This Happen?

Historians once thought that Abraham was probably a contemporary of the great Babylonian king Hammurabi, who is famous for his code of laws. Some even thought that perhaps the Amraphel, king of Shinar, mentioned in Genesis 14 might be Hammurabi. But best estimates now place the famous Babylonian king on the throne a few years later, in the first half of the eighteenth century B.C.—which would have been near the very end of Abraham's life.

To help put this in perspective, consider what was happening in other parts of the world during Abraham's lifetime. On the island of Crete, the Middle Minoan Culture was in its heyday. The great palace at Knossos, famous for having had indoor plumbing with toilets superior to any in Europe before modern times, was possibly being built while Abraham was living in a tent in the oak grove at Mamre. The Minoan culture would thrive for 550 years prior to being replaced by the Mycenaean Greek Culture. Another thousand years after that, Hellenic culture would come to its full flower in Athens in the age of Socrates, Plato, and Pericles.

Perhaps two hundred years before Abraham's birth, an area around the Yellow River Valley in China was first brought under one government, known as the Hsia (or Xia) Dynasty. It would last for about 450 years, and then be replaced by the Shang Dynasty, which would endure for nearly seven centuries—down to the time of Israel's first king, Saul. Speaking of Israel, Abraham must have been born almost a millennium before Solomon, who took the throne at the death of David in about 971 B.C.

Egypt was already an old civilization in Abraham's day, ruled by what is now known as the Twelfth Dynasty. If Abraham's trip to Egypt took him to Giza, he would have seen the Great Pyramid, which had already been standing for seven centuries!

In the Indus Valley, part of modern Pakistan, a civilization known as the Harappan Culture had been in existence since about the time the pyramids were being built. It disappeared mysteriously about two hundred years after Abraham's birth.

In England, people had been gathering for several centuries at a manmade circular ditch at the place we know as Stonehenge. The huge circle of stones that people still visit today may have been erected at about the time Abraham was building his little stone altar at Bethel.

JOURNEY TO MORIAH

The Roman Republic wouldn't even be a twinkle in anyone's eye for another fourteen hundred years, and the Empire wouldn't be founded until nearly five hundred years after that.

In the area around Babylon, Sargon I's Akkadian Empire had blossomed and died nearly three hundred years before Abraham's birth. Closer to home, the Third Dynasty of Ur had expanded the influence of Abraham's birth city to control almost all of Mesopotamia 150 years before the patriarch was born. But the dynasty had been overrun by the Elamites and Amorites when Abraham's father, Terah, was just a young man.

You're probably wondering how all this fits in with the genealogical records in Genesis. My Bible lists only ten generations lasting about 350 years between the time of the Flood and the birth of Abraham. How could all these civilizations have flourished in widespread parts of the world in so little time?

That's one of the questions anyone studying the chronology of the biblical stories has to consider carefully. Personally, I've come to the conclusion that the lists found in Genesis and some other biblical books are probably "high-point" lists. In other words, rather than listing every single member of every single generation, the lists focus on the most important names— the ones people would remember, or the ones who had an especially important part in history. When that is done, some generations get left out. So, adding together the life spans listed doesn't necessarily give the full picture of the amount of time that elapsed between the Flood and Abraham's birth.

Try this if you're an American: List as many presidents, in order, as you can remember. Did you remember all forty-plus? Are you sure you got them all in the right order? And oh, by the way, did you list the years they served too? If you're like most people, you probably can list only a dozen or so of the presidents, those who had a major impact on history— men like George Washington, Thomas Jefferson, and Abraham Lincoln.

It seems likely to me that this is the kind of list we find in Genesis as well. I don't think God ever intended that the genealogical lists be used to formulate a chronology of earth's history. The lists are there to remind us of great people and what they did—just like the list of all the great heroes of faith in Hebrews 11.

Abraham is one of those heroes—perhaps the greatest of them all. And his story is the start of something very big and very important. It

When Did All This Happen?

began in Ur of the Chaldees, which most archaeologists identify with a site on the Euphrates River halfway between Babylon and the Persian Gulf. In Abraham's time, Ur was an important city, but not as influential as it had been a few years earlier when it was the capital of the powerful Third Dynasty of Ur, which ruled most of modern Iraq and parts of Iran. By the time Abraham left Ur, much of Mesopotamia was controlled by two neighboring cities, Isin and Larsa. And before long, things would change drastically as Babylon, to the north, grew in power under Hammurabi's rule and gained control of an even larger area than Ur had ruled—incidentally, a fact that helps us pinpoint the time of Abraham. The story found in Genesis 14 must have happened before Hammurabi brought all of Mesopotamia under his control in the middle of the eighteenth century B.C. Don't confuse this Babylonian kingdom with the one we read about in Daniel and the historical and prophetical books of the Bible. That empire arose about thirteen hundred years later, under Nabopolassar and his famous son Nebuchadnezzar.

There have actually been three major empires centered in Babylon or its immediate vicinity. The first was the Akkadian Empire founded by Sargon I (also known as Sargon of Agade—a city near Babylon that has never been identified by archaeologists), whose dates are usually given as 2371 to 2316 B.C. Hammurabi (1792–1750 B.C.) is the best known ruler of the Old Babylonian Kingdom, which was founded in about 1900 B.C. but didn't grow large or powerful until fairly late in Hammurabi's reign. It came to an end in 1595 B.C. The New Babylonian Kingdom rose to prominence under Nebuchadnezzar's father and had a brief florescence lasting from about 626 to 539 B.C.

Abraham's life fits neatly between empires, in a time when no single nation held firm control of the areas God led him to wander in. It was a time of opportunity, and Abraham was the man who had the faith to seize the day.

I find it fascinating to view Abraham's life and other Bible stories within their historical setting—so fascinating, in fact, that I spent several years developing a set of Bible timeline charts that colorfully illustrate how the Bible stories fit into history. If you're interested in this type of thing, please stop by my Web page at <www.biblelights.com> and look at the charts.